New Insights into the Provision of Health
Services in Indonesia

New Insights into the Provision of Health Services in Indonesia

A Health Workforce Study

Claudia Rokx, John Giles, Elan Satriawan,
Puti Marzoeki, Pandu Harimurti, and
Elif Yavuz

THE WORLD BANK
Washington, D.C.

1818 H Street NW
Washington DC 20433
Telephone: 202-473-1000
Internet: www.worldbank.org
E-mail: feedback@worldbank.org

ISBN: 978-0-8213-8298-1
eISBN: 978-0-8213-8299-8
DOI: 10.1596/978-0-8213-8298-1

Library of Congress Cataloging-in-Publication Data

New insights into the provision of health services in Indonesia : a health work force study / Claudia Rokx . . . [et al.].
    p. ; cm. — (Directions in development)
  Includes bibliographical references and index.
  ISBN 978-0-8213-8298-1 (alk. paper) — ISBN 978-0-8213-8299-8
  1. Public health—Indonesia. 2. Public health personnel—Indonesia. 3. Medical personnel—Indonesia.
I. Rokx, Claudia, 1964- II. World Bank. III. Series: Directions in development (Washington, D.C.)
  [DNLM: 1. Health Manpower—Indonesia. 2. Health Policy—Indonesia. 3. Health Services—supply & distribution—Indonesia. 4. Health Services Accessibility—Indonesia. 5. Quality of Health Care—Indonesia. W 76 N5313 2010]
  RA541.I55N49 2010
  362.109598—dc22

                                                                                          2010002472

Cover photo: Antara foto
Cover design: Naylor Design, Washington, D.C.

Contents

Box

Figures

Tables

Foreword

Indonesia has made improving the access to health workers, especially in rural areas, and improving the quality of health providers key priority areas of its next five-year development plan. Significant steps and policy changes were taken to improve the distribution of the health workforce, in particular the contracted doctors program and later the contracted midwives program, but few studies have been undertaken to measure the actual impact of these policies and programs.

This study makes an effort to start reviewing the impacts of past policies and policy changes. It links the changes in supply and quality of health workers to past policies in the area of health workforce but also to changes in financing and civil service reforms. In addition, very important aspects of health professional education and changes in demand for services are reviewed.

The study findings show Indonesia's progress in increasing the number of health workers and providing better access to health services, especially in remote areas. Although midwifery services are well distributed between urban and rural areas, general practitioners are not deployed equally. The study also presents interesting results regarding changes over time in health providers' ability to diagnose and treat in the areas of prenatal, child curative, and adult curative care, using the Indonesia Family Life Survey.

Based on the findings of the study and consultations with the government and with stakeholders in the area, suggestions for policy changes, further research topics, and areas for experimentation are laid out.

The study described here provides valuable inputs to the government of Indonesia's next five-year national development plan and the ongoing reforms of the health workforce that are part of the overall health sector reform, with the objective of strengthening Indonesia's health system to improve health outcomes. The information and results in this study provide important inputs to future work on health provider skills mix and composition to adapt to the changes in demand and need created by the demographic, epidemiological, and nutritional transitions that are taking place in Indonesia.

Nina Sardjunani
Deputy Minister for Human Resources and Cultural Affairs
State Ministry for National Development Planning
(*Bappenas*)

Emmanuel Y. Jimenez
Sector Director
East Asia Human Development Sector
World Bank

Acknowledgments

This report was prepared by a team led by Claudia Rokx (Lead Health Specialist, East Asia Human Development Sector Department, EASHD). The main authors are Claudia Rokx, John Giles (Senior Labor Economist, DECRG), Elan Satriawan (Assistant Professor, School of Economics, Gadjah Mada University), Puti Marzoeki (Senior Health Specialist, EASHD), Pandu Harimurti (Health Specialist, EASHD), and Elif Yavuz (doctoral student, Harvard University School of Public Health).

The final report benefited from the comments of Magnus Lindelow (Senior Economist, EASHD), Jishnu Das (Senior Economist, DECRG), and Marko Vujicic (Health Economist, HDNHE). Other World Bank staff members and professionals who provided comments and assistance during the writing of the study include Eko Pambudi (Research Analyst, EASHD), George Schieber (Senior Health Policy Adviser, consultant), Ajay Tandon (Senior Economist, HDNHE), William Wallace (Lead Economist, EASPR), Jed Friedman (Senior Economist, DECRG), Christoph Kurowski (Sector Leader, LCSHD), Kenneth Chomitz (Senior Adviser, IEGWB), Pablo Gottret (Lead Economist, SASHD), Mariam Claeson (Program Coordinator, SASHD), Anna Revenga (Sector Director, PREMPR), Sandy Lieberman (Lead Health Economist, consultant), and Agnes Soucat (Adviser, AFTHE). Editorial assistance was provided by Chris Stewart and Mary Fisk.

On the government side, the team coordinated closely with, and bene-fited from, the valuable inputs, reviews, and consultations of, Nina Sardjunani (Deputy for Human Resources and Culture, *Bappenas*), Prof. Fasli Jalal (Director General of Higher Education, Ministry of National Education), Bambang Giatno (Chair of Board for Development and Empowerment of HHR), Arum Atmawikarta (Director for Health and Community Nutrition, *Bappenas*), Abdurrahman (Head of Center for HRH Planning and Empowerment, Ministry of Health [MoH]), Sri Wahyuni (Center for Health Development, MoH), Susilawaty (Head, Division of Program and Human Resources, Center for Medical Education Personnel, MoH), Hikmandari (Public Communication Department, MoH), Tati Suryati and Martuti Budiharto (Center for Research and Health Development, MoH), and Arsita Pudji Rahardjo (Special Assistant to the Director General, Higher Education, Ministry of National Education), and from professional associations—Prof. Hardyanto Soebono (Chairman of Doctor Council), Prof. Achir Yani S. Hamid (Chairman, PP–PPNI), and Harni Koesno (Chairman, PP–IBI). The team also acknowledges the assis-tance of a number of academics, including Prof. Laksono Trisnantoro of Gadjah Mada University, and Mardiati Nadjib of the University of Indonesia, and of Firman Witoelar of SurveyMeter.

The team also benefited from inputs and assistance from the donor partners in health in Indonesia, in particular, Rosalia Sciortino (Health Adviser, AusAID), Ainsley Hemming (Program Development Specialist, AusAID), Khyn Win Win Sue (Child Survival and Development Cluster, UNICEF), and Franz von Roenne (Principal Health Adviser, Gesellschaft fur Technische Zusammenarbeit [GTZ]).

The study was conducted under the general guidance of Joachim von Amsberg (Country Director, Indonesia), Emmanuel Jimenez (Sector Director, East Asia Human Development Sector Department), Juan Pablo Uribe (Health Nutrition and Population Sector Manager), and William Wallace (Lead Economist, Poverty Reduction and Economic Management).

This study could not have been conducted without the generous sup-port from the Australian government's aid agency, AusAID, and the UK Department for International Development (DFID).

Abbreviations

Askeskin	*Asuransi Kesehatan Masyarakat Miskin* (Health Insurance for the Poor)
Bappenas	*Badan Perencanaan Pembangunan Nasional* (State Ministry for National Development Planning / Indonesian National Development Agency)
BDD	*Bidan di Desa* (village midwife)
BKN	*Badan Kepegawaian Negara* (National Civil Service Agency)
BPPSDMK	*Badan Pengembangan dan Pemberdayaan Sumber Daya Manusia Kesehatam* (National Institute of Health / Human Resources Development and Empowerment)
BPS	*Badan Pusat Statistik* (Central Bureau of Statistics)
DEPKES	*Departmen Kesehatan* (Ministry of Health)
Desa	village
Desa Siaga	alert village
DHS	Demographic and Health Survey
EAP	East Asia and Pacific
GDP	gross domestic product
GDS	Governance and Decentralization Survey
GNI	gross national income

IDI	*Ikatan Dokter Indonesia* (Indonesian Medical Association)
IFLS	Indonesia Family Life Survey
IMMPACT	Initiative for Maternal Mortality Programme Assessment
IMR	infant mortality rate
Jamkesmas	*Jaminan Kesehatan Masyarakat* (Community Health Insurance Scheme)
KKI	*Konsil Kedokteran Indonesia* (Indonesian Medical Council)
MENPAN	Ministry of State Apparatus Reform
MMR	maternal mortality ratio
MoH	Ministry of Health
MoNE	Ministry of National Education
NCD	noncommunicable disease
OTC	over the counter
PCE	per capita expenditure
PODES	*Potensi Desa* (Survey of Village Potential)
Polindes	*pondok bersalin desa* (village midwife)
Posyandu	*pos pelayanan terpadu* (integrated health services post)
PTT	*pegawai tidak tetap* (contract employee)
Puskesmas	*pusat kesehatan masyarakat* (public health center)
Pustu	*puskesmas pembantu* (auxiliary health center)
Riskesdas	*riset kesehatan dasar* (basic health research)

Overview

This book is part of the inputs prepared at the request of the government of Indonesia's national development agency, *Bappenas*, to inform the development of the next National Development Plan 2010–14. Other inputs include reports on health financing, fiscal space for health, health public expenditure review, and assessments of maternal health and pharmaceuticals.

Context and Background

Over the past decade, a number of important reforms and transitions have taken place in Indonesia and in the health sector in particular. They include the decentralization of responsibilities for service delivery to the district level; policy reforms of the incentive structure for health providers, especially regarding compensation for service in remote areas; and policy changes to increase the supply of midwives in rural and remote areas. Demographic and epidemiological transitions have also occurred, causing changes in the pattern of disease prevalence in Indonesia. With chronic disease on the rise, Indonesia now faces a double burden of disease. Resources for the health sector have steadily increased since the financial crisis in 1996 but remain low in comparison to those in other low-middle-income countries (World Bank 2008). Private health practitioners are now providing a large share of health care, and private institutions such as medical and midwifery schools are educating a large share of the incoming health workforce.

The Indonesian government is committed to improving both financial and physical access to quality health care. Past and ongoing reforms aim to improve the supply, quality, and utilization of care to produce better health outcomes, particularly in remote areas and among the poor. Financial protection against catastrophic expenditures has improved substantially since the introduction of the health insurance program for the poor, *Askeskin/Jamkesmas*. Furthermore, a number of legal acts have been used as the basis for improving the quality of Indonesian physicians. The Medical Practice Act (2004) supported the establishment of the Indonesian Medical Council (KKI), which produced standards for physician competencies and medical education in 2006. Given the varying capacities of Indonesian medical schools, however, the standards are not implemented consistently, and, as a consequence, large and growing variation in quality exists among schools and their graduates.

The Importance of the Indonesian Health Workforce

This study is concerned with the impact of the above-mentioned reforms on the Indonesian health care workforce. It is an area with great potential for improving health outcomes but also one that is complex and challenging. In Indonesia, some key health workforce challenges relate to (a) limited supply of health care providers at the primary as well as the hospital level; (b) payment systems that do not encourage an optimal distribution of health workers, equitable access to care, and efficient provision of services; (c) shortcomings in the quality of maternal and child care, as well as adult care; (d) lack of oversight and effective licensing in an expanding private health sector; and (e) continuing challenges related to planning, recruitment, and retention of health workers, particularly since decentralization.

Given the slow progress in improving health outcomes and limited evidence linking health performance and the health workforce in Indonesia, a pressing need exists to make more information available about past experiences to inform future policy changes. This study seeks to contribute to the government of Indonesia's broader health system assessment by answering key health workforce questions. It examines changes in the supply and quality of health service providers and practitioners and, where possible, links those changes with past and ongoing reforms. Based on these analyses, the study provides policy suggestions for the areas in need of reform.

Summary of Findings

Study findings highlight the importance not only of improving the supply of health care, but also of improving quality, so as to improve health outcomes. Over the period studied, important gains in the determinants of health outcomes have occurred in Indonesia. At the same time, however, the study shows that Indonesia, despite the significant gains, continues to suffer from serious challenges in the number and distribution, and in particular the quality, of its health workers.

Supply of Health Facilities and Health Practitioners

Indonesia's health policy, "Healthy Indonesia 2010," which emphasizes giving priority to primary health care and boosting expenditures for health, has had a positive impact, with overall increases in public facilities and workforce numbers since the mid-1990s. The increase in the supply of health workers reflects the government's attention to increasing the supply of health services, especially in remote and rural areas, as well as significant increases in the public budget for health since 2004. It also reflects the growing business opportunities and interest in the profession. For example, in 2003–04 medical schools received more than 80,000 applications, though they only had capacity to take in 4,700 new students. The number of midwifery and nursing schools has increased, and by 2008, 465 midwifery and 682 nursing schools in Indonesia were producing about 10,000 midwives and 34,000 nurses every year. Since decentralization, local governments have focused on increasing the availability of health care by giving priority to the construction of new health centers, or *puskesmas*, and increasing community access to services through auxiliary health centers, or *pustu*.

Although the number of physicians and the ratio of physicians to population in all provinces and in rural areas have increased, deployment practices and inequitable distribution remain serious concerns. The recently initiated policy requiring six months of mandatory service in a remote area for new graduates, which allows easier access to specialist education and includes a lucrative payment schedule, has resulted in more physicians taking up posts in those areas. However, past deployment policies have not sufficiently addressed distribution concerns.

More important, although the research undertaken for this study allows for a distinction between urban and rural areas, the data sources used do not always include Indonesia's most remote areas, some of which are likely to be seriously underserved (see chapter 1, in the section Data and Methodology). In addition, those remote areas that are included might not be appropriately observed, since the rural category is substantial and comprises settlements that range in size (and workforce supply) from periurban to very remote and hard to reach.

Since 1996, the average number of physicians per *puskesmas* has grown. At the same time, more *puskesmas* have no doctor, especially in rural areas, confirming distributional concerns. Moreover, the gap between rural and urban areas in the ratio of private physicians to population has increased, and at present the supply of private physician services is far greater in urban areas. Availability of midwifery services has also increased in both urban and rural areas since 1996. The increase in urban areas was very significant but may be explained by large numbers of former village midwives returning to urban areas after completing their service under the village midwife, or *Bidan Di Desa* (BDD), program. Unfortunately, information on nurses is substantially lacking, in terms of both overall numbers and distribution, limiting analysis of their supply and utilization.

The decentralization of health services may permit a more efficient planning and recruitment system. A lack of clarity on roles and responsibilities with respect to hiring and firing, however, has limited the impact of decentralization in this respect, so that a more even distribution of health workers has not occurred. The central government is still heavily involved in the recruitment, deployment, and financing of public doctors working under civil service contracts. The lack of progress on civil service reform further impedes more efficient planning at all levels. At the same time, local governments have received more autonomy in the provision of resources for relocations and performance incentives, which can have a substantial impact at the district level.

Growth in the number of private physician practices in communities is associated with increased utilization of health services by poorer members of the community. The poor are more likely to use the public *puskesmas* as the private sector grows. This suggests that the increase in supply of health service providers reduces congestion costs in the public *puskesmas*, while also sorting more affluent members of the community to private practices.

Finally, it seems that allowing and encouraging dual practice has significantly increased the supply of health services, including in rural areas.

The lack of oversight over private health services is of concern, however, and needs urgent attention. Little information has been gathered on actual hours spent in public service. A large part of almost all health workers' income comes from providing private services. Where private services are plentiful, it may well be that health care workers are spending less time in public service. This may lead to inefficiencies in the use of public budgets for health, a large part of which is for salaries.

Quality of Health Facilities and Health Practitioners

The government of Indonesia has given attention to improving the quality of health providers through additional training, especially in the area of maternal health. For example, in 1997 the government began an in-service, competency-based training program in skills ranging from normal birth to emergency obstetric care. New requirements for midwifery training were also introduced that changed basic midwifery training from one year after vocational nursing school, to a three-year, post–high school, diploma program. The Indonesian Medical Association (IDI) also piloted a training program in emergency obstetric care for general practitioners in early 2000. That program was discontinued in 2005, when a ministerial decree allowed family practice doctors with additional training to provide emergency obstetric care in remote areas. These and other initiatives and policy changes would be expected to have improved the quality of health providers.

Overall quality of services provided by public and private facilities and freestanding practitioners has improved over time in all provinces for prenatal care, child curative care, and adult care. However, the improvements in quality—measured as ability to diagnose and treat—were marginal, and overall quality remains low, with health workers only responding correctly to about half of the standard questions and procedures in the diagnostic vignettes presented in the most recent Indonesia Family Life Survey (IFLS).[1] Although quality is not perfectly measured by vignettes, the information on health provider knowledge available from this source is the latest and most reliable evidence available. Moreover, these data are representative across regions for different types of health providers and the three types of care. Changes in provider quality over time can be analyzed, as the 1997 IFLS used the same vignette module.

Increasing the number of private sector physicians per 100,000 population is associated with improvement in the average diagnostic ability of all facilities. The changes in prenatal care, child curative care, and adult curative care scores from diagnostic and treatment vignettes are all positively correlated with changes in the number of private physician practices in the community. These relationships are statistically significant for prenatal and child curative care.

No evidence is found indicating that dual practice opportunities lead to decline in the diagnostic and treatment abilities of health care workers in the *puskesmas*.[2] One worry regarding the growth in the number of private physician practices is that they may have a detrimental effect on the quality of care in the *puskesmas*. The study found that the diagnostic ability of health providers available in the *puskesmas* did not deteriorate with growth of the private sector. Although this is a positive finding, further study of physicians' use of their time in public and private services is important for a more complete understanding of the costs and benefits of dual practice in Indonesia.

The diagnostic as well as the treatment practices of doctors for prenatal care are rated less highly than those of midwives, based on analysis of detailed vignette scores. Only 28 percent of doctors checked a patient's blood pressure and fewer than 6 percent checked for protein in urine during a prenatal visit. Much of the training of the past decade has been focused on improving midwives. Nevertheless, ongoing quality concerns exist regarding midwives' ability to provide care and accurate diagnoses. Given that the use of midwifery services has increased more than use of any other service, particularly among the poor, further quality improvements at this provider level are still necessary, despite their performance advantage over doctors and nurses. There is little difference between midwives' practices and *puskesmas* in terms of prenatal care; prenatal care provided by private nurses shows rather low quality scores.

Private physicians compare favorably to *puskesmas* health workers when it comes to child curative care, and yet, as with prenatal care, the overall scores of all types of service providers are on the low side. For example, as part of the child curative care vignette, an indicative question is whether the health worker asks about the nature of the stool when a child has diarrhea. Only 42 percent of *puskesmas* health workers and 43 percent of private physicians indicated that they would ask this question, and even fewer private nurses and midwives would do so. Oral rehydration fluids are administered by 79 percent of *puskesmas* and *pustu* health workers and by 74 percent of private physicians, but by only 41 percent of private midwives.

Differences between *puskesmas* and private physicians are less pronounced for adult curative care. Nurses compare more favorably on this vignette than on others, with midwives scoring the lowest in this care category. Overall adult care has improved marginally, in line with improvements in prenatal and child care. Further analysis of average vignette scores by competency category (in quintiles) indicated no major differences in average quintile vignette scores between public and private practitioners, but all improved over time. At the same time, even for the highest competency category, average scores were only above 90 percent for child curative care.

Private practice physicians appeared to focus less on providing public health services, such as measles immunizations for children and tetanus for pregnant women, in 2007. Fewer than 12 percent of physicians had vaccines available in their private practices, whereas more than 22 percent did in 1997. Tetanus availability at midwives' private practices remained at just under 60 percent, which is much better than for physicians but still far from complete coverage. Overall public health functions and quality of public health interventions appear to have decreased and require urgent attention, not only from the central government but also from local governments. Tuberculosis treatment services have been reduced sharply in private settings and *pustu* (auxiliary health centers), from more than half of all *pustu* and 56 percent of private physicians in 1997. In comparison, more than 95 percent of *puskesmas* continued to provide tuberculosis treatment in 2007.

Studies have shown that the quality of health professional education, especially for midwives and nurses, is lagging in Indonesia (Hennessy et al. 2006; World Bank 2008). The current regulatory framework governing the quality of these institutions is weak. Of particular concern is the rapid growth of new schools in the absence of a proper credentialing process. Although reforms and increased investment to address the quality of education for the health professions are ongoing, results will not be reflected in increased quality in the short term.[3] Not only is preservice training lagging, but internships to allow practical clinical skills to be obtained are also in short supply and of poor quality.

Implications for Utilization of Health Services
The ultimate beneficiaries of improvements in the supply and quality of services are the people, and they have a choice. First of all, people choose whether or not to seek care when ill; second, they make a choice about which provider to consult. One would expect that with more supply and better quality, people would choose to make more use of their preferred provider. This study therefore looks at changes in utilization and, where possible, does so with correlates of changes in trends in supply and quality.

Recently the government of Indonesia introduced its program of health insurance for the poor, *Askeskin/Jamkesmas*, which removed financial barriers to care and appears to have induced people to seek more care. This reform should be kept in mind when interpreting the changes in utilization, supply, and quality.

Between 1997 and 2007, overall use of both inpatient and outpatient health services among those who report illness increased. Usage rates rose from 20.5 percent in 1997 to 23.0 percent in 2007 and from 2.2 percent to 3.2 percent for inpatient utilization over the same period. The largest increase in overall utilization occurred among the poorest quintiles. At the same time, a large proportion of the population forgoes any treatment at all, and that percentage increased from 23 percent to 27 percent over the period. Most people in Indonesia—two-thirds of the population—rely on self-treatment when ill.

As expected, richer households are more likely to seek health care when ill. Those households also have higher education levels, which, like higher income levels, are also associated with greater use. However, utilization among the poorest, especially women, has increased considerably. The poor in Indonesian communities are more likely to choose public providers, while the relatively affluent are more likely to seek care from the private sector. This appears to be particularly true in rural areas.

Further analysis indicates that the number of private sector providers per 100,000 population is positively associated with the use of public sector facilities by the poor. Increasing the number of private sector physicians per 100,000 is also associated with improvement in the average quality of services. Importantly, there is no evidence that dual practice opportunities are leading to a decline in the diagnostic and treatment abilities of health care workers in the *puskesmas*.

Policy Suggestions

The findings described above from the latest available data suggest a number of important policy options for consideration by Indonesian policy makers and academics:

Policy with Regard to Supply and Distribution

- Monitoring and evaluating current deployment policy appear crucial to ascertain whether it is an effective long-term strategy to maintain quality health workers in remote areas. The current government's deployment policy—a mandatory six-month service period in a remote area, combined with financial and nonfinancial incentives—appears to have had a positive effect in the short term. But while short-duration postings of young providers in a location may be sufficient to improve people's access to curative care, promotive and preventive care requires a more stable presence in one location by providers able to understand the particular context and develop relationships with their patients.

- In addition to evaluation of the current policy of reduced mandatory service, it is highly recommended that the government of Indonesia continue to develop and experiment with other incentive schemes to improve deployment and ensure the long-term provision of quality health services in rural and remote areas. Appendix 6 provides a listing of various types of financial and nonfinancial incentives, as an illustration of possibilities.[4] Gadjah Mada University is conducting some promising initial experiments with nonfinancial incentives, such as creating a more attractive working environment by bringing together teams with an effective skills mix, which merit more attention and evaluation. And recently, international focus on deployment issues has turned to the creation of a "rural pipeline" of providers by targeting recruitment to rural areas through measures ranging from creating increased interest in the health professions in secondary schools to developing specific rural health curriculums in health professional schools. Experiments and pilots could be developed to evaluate the appropriateness of these approaches in Indonesia.

- The private health sector should be included in planning and budgeting considerations to ensure more optimal use of existing resources. This could include contracting out services and promoting health insurance schemes that equalize reimbursement rates for public and private providers of health care services. The private sector provides about one-half of all health services in Indonesia and continues to grow.

- For improvement of planning and needs-based licensing processes, it is recommended that more comprehensive data be collected on who works where, both publicly and privately. At present, data collection is fragmented and incomplete. Local governments' current process for licensing new private health practices is inadequate and is not based on assessment of need; nor does it sufficiently take existing health services into account, especially those provided privately. Finally, linking planning with overall civil service reforms is imperative.

- More thorough analysis of physician hours spent in public and in private facilities and the cost-effectiveness of allowing dual practice is needed to gain a better understanding of the impact of dual practice and to adapt policy where necessary. Indonesia's impressive gains in access to health services are explained, in part, by dual practice. Coupled with removal of financial barriers, dual practice has increased the use both of services at public facilities, *puskesmas* and *pustu*, and of services provided privately by physicians, midwives, and nurses. Although the study found no evidence that dual practice has a negative impact on the knowledge of health care providers at the *puskesmas,* it did not address other important dimensions of the quality of services, such as effort and time spent with patients. Analysis of both physicians' knowledge and their use of time in public and private practice would provide a more complete picture of whether dual practice opportunities have a negative impact on the quality of care available in the *puskesmas.*

- More understanding is needed about the impacts of the so-called sorting of patients in which the poor make more use of public services while the more affluent seek care at private facilities. The initial indication is that the existence of dual practice has contributed to the sorting of patients. That may have a positive effect on efficiency, as long as the non-poor continue to support the public system. Questions regarding efficiency gains through higher-priced private provision, as well as implications for quality in both the public and private sectors, require further study. The information from available surveys, however, does not allow an analysis of the hours and level of effort spent providing public and private services.

- It is highly recommended that public funds and efforts applied to ensuring an adequate supply of health workers in underserved areas and for the poor be reviewed. Use of public health services has decreased substantially since the 1997–98 economic and financial crisis, and although some increases have occurred since 2000, utilization remains far below the earlier levels. Instead, utilization of private health services, especially those of private midwives and nurses, has increased. A large part of public spending goes to operate public facilities that have seen declining rates of utilization, especially by richer quintiles, in places where private services are available. Moreover, the continuing one-size-fits-all service delivery strategy is inadequate because it does not take into account the great diversity among regions in Indonesia.

- Indonesia should consider allowing the privileging of certain interventions by nurses and midwives in rural and remote areas. Nurses and midwives continue to be among the primary providers of health services for the poor in remote and rural areas. As the analysis of changes in utilization shows, most people, when ill, now seek treatment from nurses and midwives. Yet the low quality of nurses providing private services, measured as ability to diagnose and treat, is alarming and needs urgent attention.

- The overall planning of staffing in the health sector needs to be adapted to local needs and to changes in policy and should take ongoing transitions into account. For example, in areas where many private-practice physicians are providing curative care, the lack of a physician in a *puskesmas* may not be of concern, as long as the poor have access to the private physicians. Access could be achieved through changing the reimbursement policies of *Jamkesmas* to include services by private physicians.

- The demographic, epidemiological, and nutritional transitions that are occurring in Indonesia will require adaptations in the skills mix, numbers, and distribution of health workers and should be taken into account when developing the reforms suggested here.

Policy with Regard to Quality
- For Indonesia to improve the quality of its health services, the regulatory framework that governs the providers and the quality of their training needs urgent attention. Experiments and pilot programs applying different provider payment mechanisms are also highly recommended. Much of the improvement in quality of service is embedded in two parts of the health system: the regulatory framework and provider payment incentives. The increasing number of private sector providers, without adequate oversight of the quality of the services they provide, and the marginal improvements in health services despite the growing attention to training for providers suggest that current policies need to be revisited.

Specific actions include (a) establishing competency and education standards and a regulatory body for nurses and midwives; (b) rationalizing the accreditation of public and private health professional training institutions and ensuring that it is competency focused; and (c) encouraging the professional associations to improve the continuing education program and to link it to licensing.

- Beyond these, a concrete step that the government could consider is limiting the recruitment of doctors as civil servants to those who have been certified according to national standards. That will ensure the efficient use of public resources, as well as motivate health care providers to obtain accreditation and certification. Many providers are graduating from schools that are not accredited, or are insufficiently accredited, and the certification process is lacking as well. An urgent need also exists to better control the establishment of new schools and link them to the accreditation system.

- The method of certifying physicians, nurses, and midwives should be strengthened to measure skills in provision of care, not only knowledge, as is currently the practice. Accreditation and certification standards and processes for facilities should also be improved. A needs-based master plan should also be considered, covering the whole country and including both public and private facilities and manpower. Private sector involvement in medical and paramedical education also warrants strong public sector oversight to ensure the quality of services.

Notes

1. The IFLS is a data source available at http://www.rand.org/labor/FLS/IFLS/.
2. A negative and significant coefficient on change in number of physician practices per 100,000 could be driven by the fact that physicians with side practices were not in their public health clinic offices at the time that enumerators showed up.
3. The World Bank cofinances the Health Professional Education Quality project, managed by the director general for higher education at Indonesia's Ministry of National Education (MoNE). It aims at strengthening the quality assurance policies governing the education of health professionals in Indonesia through (a) rationalizing accreditation of public and private health professional training institutions and ensuring that it is competency focused; (b) developing national competency standards and testing procedures for certification and

licensing of health professionals; and (c) building institutional capacity to employ results-based grants to encourage the use of accreditation and certification standards in the development of medical school quality.

4. For guidance on developing an incentive package, see *Guidelines: Incentives for Health Professionals*, Joint Initiative of the International Council of Nurses, International Hospital Federation, International Pharmaceutical Federation, World Confederation of Physical Therapy, World Dental Federation, and the World Medical Association, 2008, at http://www.who.int/workforcealliance/documents/Incentives_Guidelines%20EN.pdf.

References

Hennessy, D., C. Hicks, A. Hilan, and Y. Kawonal. 2006. "The Training and Development Needs of Nurses in Indonesia." Paper 3 of 3. *Human Resources for Health* 4: 10. http://www.human-resources-health/content/4/1/10.

World Bank. 2008. *Investing in Indonesia's Health: Challenges and Opportunities for Future Public Spending. Health Public Expenditure Review 2008.* Jakarta: World Bank.

CHAPTER 1

Introduction

Over the past decade, a number of important reforms and transitions have taken place in Indonesia and in its health sector. With the implementation of decentralization in 2001, the responsibility for delivery of services, including health services, was delegated to the district level. Public resources for health have increased almost fourfold since 2002, but Indonesian disease outcomes still lag those of many neighboring countries (World Bank 2008). At the same time, chronic diseases and injuries are becoming more prevalent while communicable diseases remain an important part of the burden of disease, changing needs for health care services and provider skills. Finally, the implementation of Law No. 40/2004, Universal Health Insurance Coverage, will influence demand for health services and health workers.

As staffing responsibilities have evolved with decentralization, and as the number of training institutions has steadily risen, important human resource policy changes have been introduced in the health sector. The recruitment and incentive structures for health providers have undergone several changes over time, especially regarding remote area compensation. At the same time, the private health sector is expanding rapidly, and a combination of events has reduced the information that the government has about the private health sector. The regulatory framework governing human resources in the health field is weak at best, and public oversight over the training of health workers and over the private health sector is insufficient. Given the mixed performance in improving health outcomes in Indonesia and the limited evidence linking better health system performance with health workforce policies, it is apparent that health reformers need more relevant information to inform the policy-making process.

This report is part of the material prepared at the request of the government of Indonesia's national development agency, *Bappenas* (Badan Perencanaan Pembangunan Nasional, or State Ministry for National Development Planning/Indonesian National Development Agency), to inform the development of the next National Development Plan 2010–14. Other inputs include reports on health financing and fiscal space for health assessment, a health public expenditure review, and assessments of maternal health and pharmaceuticals (see, for example, Rokx et al. 2009; World Bank 2008, 2009a, 2009b). This report and those earlier inputs contribute to a comprehensive review of the health sector in Indonesia and will inform the development of the next medium-term plan, as well as the health reform agenda that will help the health sector adapt to the new needs of its health system.

Rationale and Objectives of This Report

Much has been written about the public health workforce in Indonesia, the problems and constraints of managing it, and the limited impact of previous reforms in improving access to high-quality health care. Research specifically on the private health workforce is limited and focuses on the period predating the decentralization reforms of 2001. The most comprehensive review and guidance for the government were provided in the 1994 study *Indonesia's Health Work Force* (World Bank 1994), but that study was written in a very different context, before Indonesia's reform period of democratization and decentralization commenced. More recent work on decentralization was performed by the Center of Health Service Management of Gadjah Mada University and other partners in health policy research in Indonesia. Another analysis focusing on decentralization was carried out in 2002 (World Bank 2002), and more recently an overview paper, *Indonesia's Physicians, Midwives, and Nurses* (World Bank 2009b), was produced.

Very little analytical work on the health workforce and the impact of policy changes has been undertaken since decentralization, with the exception of one study of a 2006 policy change concerning the contracting of public physicians (Ruswendi 2007). That study demonstrated that shortening the mandatory service period under one of the government's contracting programs, the so-called PTT program,[1] from three years to six months attracted many health workers to remote areas. Recently, additional microstudies have focused on programs designed to attract midwives to remote areas under the Initiative for Maternal Mortality Programme Assessment (IMMPACT),[2] to which this report will refer in relevant sections.

The quality and distribution of health care workers, as well as the incentives presented to them, affect the overall performance of the health system. Performance will be measured in health outcomes, financial protection, consumer responsiveness, equity, efficiency, and longer-term financial sustainability. The Ministry of Health's (MoH) December 2005 platform for improving Indonesia's health sector over the next four years and beyond called for improving access to, and the quality of, human resources for health.

The overarching questions for the Indonesian health sector are whether and how the government of Indonesia can create a more equitably distributed and more effective health workforce. A more effective workforce will ensure better health outcomes and reduce inequalities in access to quality health care. It will also respond to a changing and decentralized environment; universal health insurance coverage; and the demographic, epidemiological, and nutrition transitions facing the country. This report seeks to contribute to answering the questions by examining the association between a number of important reforms and policy changes and the supply (and subsequent utilization) of health services, as well as the quality of service providers. On the basis of these analyses, the report suggests policy options and areas for future research.

Data and Methodology

The Indonesia Family Life Survey (IFLS) and the Survey of Village Potential (*Potensi Desa*, or PODES) were used to understand how past reforms and changes in human resources policies affect the supply, utilization, and quality of health care services in Indonesia.[3] Panel data from two (1997 and 2007) of the four rounds (1993, 1997, 2000, 2007) of the IFLS are exploited. They are supplemented with primary analyses and information from other existing data sources, such as the PODES from Indonesia's Central Bureau of Statistics (*Badan Pusat Statistik*, or BPS) and the Governance and Decentralization Survey (GDS), which was conducted by the World Bank and other donors in Indonesia (World Bank 2005; see appendix 1 for more details on data sources).

Trends in the distribution of *puskesmas* (pusat kesehatan masyarakat, or public health center) and *pustu* (puskesmas pembantu, or auxiliary health center) were obtained from the MoH's Health Profiles administrative database, and trends in the distribution of health practitioners from the PODES database. PODES includes census data gathered through interviews of village, or *desa*, and city block, or *kelurahan*, heads using detailed questionnaires. Each *desa* and *kelurahan* head represents a population of approximately 3,000, and each is knowledgeable about both the health workforce and the people living in the jurisdiction.

The health care facilities surveyed in the IFLS are selected according to a probability sample from among the facilities that serve households in the community. The sample is drawn from a list of facilities known by the household respondents. Health care facilities include *puskesmas* and *pustu*; community health posts (*posyandu*); and private facilities, including private clinics, doctors, nurses, paramedics, village health workers, midwives, and village midwives (*kliniks, praktek umum, perawat, paramedics, mantra, bidans,* and *bidan di desa,* respectively).

The facilities that have been reported as known to the household heads or to most knowledgeable respondents are ranked according to the number of times they are mentioned. The single most frequently reported facility is always chosen for the sample. Two to four additional facilities are selected at random from the entire listing (Beegle 2008). In each sampled health facility ($n = 2,365$), the health worker with the highest professional rank available at the time of the visit is interviewed.[4] Changes in staffing levels in *puskesmas* and *pustu* are also obtained from the IFLS.

The IFLS allows information regarding health service providers to be matched to individuals, households, and communities, facilitating analysis of how the emerging private health care sector affects access to care and the quality of care received. The IFLS further allows an analysis of changes in the structural quality and staffing of the *puskesmas* and *pustu* since 1997. Although the structural quality of health facilities is not in itself a measure of the quality of medical advice, it is a commonly used proxy (Das and Leonard 2008) and also reflects Donabedian's (1978) structural dimension of quality.[5]

Apart from using health facilities' structural characteristics as a proxy for structural quality of care, health worker vignettes from the IFLS can be used to construct indexes of provider quality. These indexes measure the diagnostic and treatment abilities of service providers without regard to their formal status as physician, nurse, or midwife. Diagnostic vignettes allow evaluation of health worker knowledge; they depict the maximum quality medical advice that workers could provide if they did all that they know how to do.[6] In a vignette, a simulated patient is presented to the health worker. The health worker's performance on the vignette is an indicator of his or her competence, skill, or ability (see Das and Leonard 2008). In this instance, these direct performance measures were employed as variables to examine how differences between providers serving the poor and those serving the nonpoor affect access to knowledgeable service providers.

Das, Hammer, and Leonard (2008) raise a concern that while vignettes measure provider knowledge, they do not pick up effort. A more qualified and knowledgeable physician may not actually exert much effort in clinical consultations, and thus health policy researchers have recently recommended combining vignettes with direct observation of health workers to examine effort as well as knowledge. One also has to ask whether effort and knowledge are correlated with those aspects of quality that are considered important. To answer those questions, the validity of vignettes can be checked for internal consistency, and the results obtained using vignettes may be compared with those obtained using more realistic instruments— ideally by direct observation (Das and Leonard 2008). Although that was not possible here, these caveats concerning the use of vignettes need to be kept in mind when interpreting the results of the analysis below.

While the distinct benefit of using the IFLS lies in the ability to exploit the panel nature of the survey to improve statistical identification when examining the effects of policy changes, IFLS–based analyses will be complemented with data from PODES and the GDS-2 (the second round of the survey in 2006). PODES data add to the study by providing information on the size of the private sector, something that cannot be distilled from IFLS data. While PODES does not differentiate between private and public practices by provider, it permits this distinction by including information on "place of work." Indicator variables that are used refer to the number of doctors and midwives living in the village, as well as the number of practices in the village, and are adjusted by population size. In addition, the GDS-2 allows the examination of other features of service delivery.

Finally, the IFLS covers only Java, Bali, Sumatra, and few other provinces outside of these regions. Provinces in the eastern part of Indonesia are not included. Although the IFLS covers about 85 percent of the Indonesian population, the poorest provinces are not included. In the following chapters, the regions are mostly classified as (a) Java and Bali; (b) Sumatra; and (c) Other Provinces (Nusa Tenggara Barat, South Kalimantan, and South Sulawesi). The sample is representative at the regional level, not the provincial level, and so comparisons can only be made at the regional level.

The Focus of the Report

The interpretation of information on the health workforce and important trends will focus on the issues outlined in the subsections below. Payment systems and incentives, decentralization, and preservice and in-service education, as well as how education institutions are accredited, are all important parts of policy affecting the health workforce. While the study does not aim to provide a rigorous evaluation of the impact of these policies and changes over time in Indonesia, discussions of likely impact will be incorporated where plausible. In addition, although overall civil service reform is crucial to any reform involving human resources, a detailed review of progress on civil service reform was beyond the scope of the study.

The study addresses five key questions:

1. How has the supply of health facilities and providers, including privately provided health services, changed over time at the national and at the regional level?
2. How has the quality of health facilities, as well as public and private health care provision, changed over time at both the national and the regional level?
3. How has the utilization of health care changed over time at the national and regional levels? More specifically, what changes in utilization are observed by type of provider and by type of facility since 1996?
4. How has the growth of the private health sector affected the supply and quality of health providers and the use of health services?
5. Finally, what is the evidence of links between changes in policies affecting access, quality, and demand, on the one hand, and health outcomes on the other?

Payment Systems and Incentives

Provider payment systems structure incentives for provision of care (Langenbrunner, Cashin, and O'Dougherty 2009). Institutional providers such as hospitals and clinics and health workers employed in institutional settings, as well as independently practicing physicians, midwives, and nurse practitioners, respond to incentives in maximizing their respective objective functions (for example, income, volume, and welfare). Provider payment systems are a critical element in health system performance and directly affect the supply and quality of care provided by facilities, their staffs, and independent practitioners.

Education and the Quality of Health Workforce Training
Education policies regarding pre-service and in-service training are important determinants of the supply, efficiency, and effectiveness of the health workforce. The costs, course length, and accessibility of medical schools have important impacts on the number of students enrolling as well as on the number of doctors, nurses, specialists, and other health workers produced. The production of health workers is also affected by the remuneration levels and additional benefits that the education is expected to yield. Accreditation policies further affect the quality of the staff trained. In-service training is particularly important for building and maintaining a health workforce familiar with the latest developments in their medical areas. The growth of private sector education institutions is also affected by oversight and regulations concerning their licensing and accreditation.

Organization and Decentralization
Changing the organization of health workforce recruitment and management and other staffing policies also has the potential to increase the efficiency and effectiveness of the health workforce and thereby population health. Administrative efficiency can arguably be improved through decentralization, as the amount of bureaucratic red tape would be reduced by involving fewer levels of government. Experimentation would be encouraged, and greater local cost consciousness might be induced. A potential drawback often mentioned, however, is the potential for higher national-level transaction costs, which can result from local administrative redundancies. However, decentralization might make allocation more efficient through greater responsiveness to local needs and priorities, while at the same time creating increased accountability through local involvement and civil participation. For that to occur requires a minimum level of local capacity, however, and points toward the risks of local-level capture (Vujicic, Ohiri, and Sparkes 2009).

Financial Protection for the Poor
The presence of a mechanism that protects consumers from financial risk also directly affects utilization and technical efficiency. In fact, another main goal of any health system is financial protection from impoverishment due to catastrophic payments for health care. The government introduced the *Askeskin/Jamkesmas* health insurance program for the poor in 2005, and by 2008, some 76 million poor and nonpoor Indonesians were projected to have coverage. The program made some changes to payment

Figure 1.1   Factors that Affect Health Outcomes

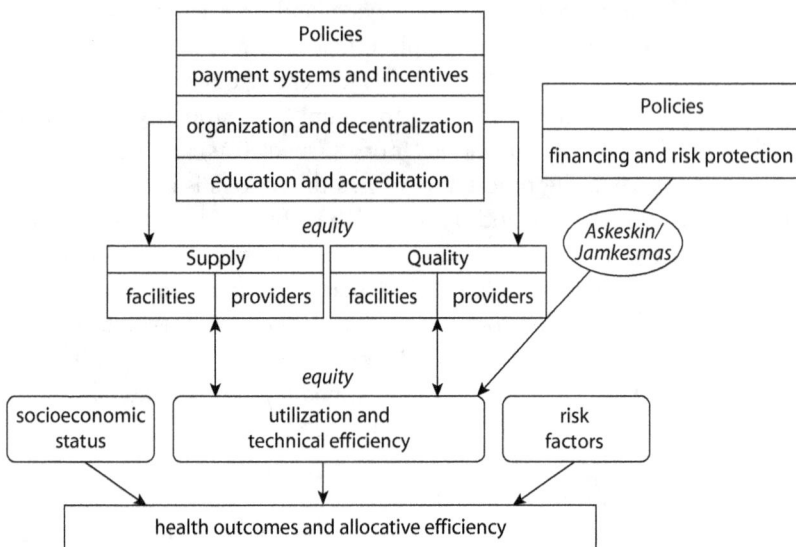

Source: Authors.

systems and removed financial barriers to the utilization of health services by the poor. Equitable access to, and quality of, health services are important determinants of health outcomes. Figure 1.1 illustrates the approach of this study to analyzing these key questions.

Structure and Outline of the Study

This rest of this study is organized into five chapters and several appendixes. Chapter 2 provides the background and context to the health workforce issues discussed in the subsequent chapters. It discusses the key challenges Indonesia faces with respect to health outcomes and describes key policies implemented over the past decade that have affected the health workforce. The areas of focus include payment systems, decentralization, education, and protection, and the government's latest program for providing insurance to the poor.

Chapter 3 explores health workforce supply issues, focusing mainly on physicians and midwives. Changes in absolute and relative numbers over time and by geographic area are discussed, as well as the ratios of various types of health workers to population and facility.

Although supply is not directly a proxy for access, these issues are put in context in chapter 4 through examination of utilization patterns over time, by provider type.

Chapter 5 addresses quality issues by a thorough examination of facilities' structural quality characteristics, such as the availability of essential medicines and clean water. Health workers' diagnostic and treatment knowledge is assessed through a discussion of survey vignette scores and changes in these indirect quality measures over the past decade.

Chapter 6 concludes with a summary of findings, which are discussed in the context of recommendations from previous work on the health workforce, as well as related health financing issues, and delineates a set of new policy options directly related to the findings of this analytical exploration.

Notes

1. The PTT (*Pegawai Tidak Tetap*, or contract employee) program was introduced in 1992. Under this program, newly graduated doctors were no longer immediately hired as civil servants but were required first to fulfill a nonrenewable, three-year appointment as "nonpermanent employees" in a province where a post became available. After completion of the PTT compulsory service, a physician could choose to (a) further specialize, (b) become a civil servant by taking a required examination, or (c) enter the private sector. The PTT program was formally abolished in 2007, and graduates can now directly enter the labor market as private providers (World Bank 2009b).

2. Initiative for Maternal Mortality Programme Assessment, under the International Research Program on Maternal Mortality.

3. The IFLS is a data source available at http://www.rand.org/labor/FLS/IFLS/; PODES is accessed at http://www.rand.org/labor/bps/podes/.

4. For the 2007 IFLS, the following respondents were interviewed: for the prenatal care vignette: general practitioners, 5 percent; midwives, 90 percent; paramedics, 5 percent; for child curative care vignette: general practitioners, 36 percent; midwives, 41 percent; nurses, 21 percent; and paramedics, 2 percent; and for adult curative care: general practitioners, 55 percent; midwives, 16 percent; nurses, 25 percent; and paramedics, 2 percent.

5. Donabedian's (1978) classic definition of quality defines it in terms of structure, process, and outcome dimensions.

6. A more refined analysis, internal validity of the vignettes, giving different weight values for each standard response, can be applied and is discussed in more detail in Das and Hammer 2005.

References

Beegle, K. G. 2008. "Health Facility and School Surveys in the Indonesia Family Life Survey." In *Are You Being Served? New Tools for Measuring Service Delivery*, ed. S. Amin, J. Das, and M. Goldstein. Washington, DC: World Bank.

Das, J., and J. Hammer. 2005. "Which Doctor? Combining Vignettes and Item Response to Measure Clinical Competence." *Journal of Development Economics* 78 (2): 348–83.

Das, J., J. Hammer, and K. Leonard. 2008. "The Quality of Medical Advice in Low-Income Countries." *Journal of Economic Perspectives* 22 (2): 93–114.

Das, J., and K. Leonard. 2008. "Using Vignettes to Measure the Quality of Health Care." In *Are You Being Served? New Tools for Measuring Service Delivery*, ed. S. Amin, J. Das, and M. Goldstein. Washington, DC: World Bank.

Donabedian, A. 1978. "The Quality of Medical Care." *Science* 200 (4344): 856–64.

Langenbrunner, J. C., C. Cashin, and S. O'Dougherty, eds. 2009. *Designing and Implementing Health Care Provider Payment Systems: How-to Manuals.* Washington, DC: World Bank.

Rokx, C., G. Schieber, P. Harimurti, A. Tandon, and A. Somanathan. 2009. *Health Financing in Indonesia: A Reform Road Map.* Washington, DC: World Bank.

Ruswendi, D. 2007. *Evaluation Study of the Deployment Policy for Contract (PTT) Doctors/Dentists in Remote Areas in 4 HWS Project Provinces: Kalimantan Barat; Kalimantan Timur; Sumatra Barat; Jambi. Year 2006–2007.* ADB Consultant Report. Manila: Asian Development Bank.

Vujicic, M., K. Ohiri, and S. Sparkes. 2009. *Working in Health: Financing and Managing the Public Sector Health Workforce.* Washington, DC: World Bank.

World Bank. 1994. *Indonesia's Health Work Force: Issues and Options.* Report No. 12835-IND. Washington, DC: World Bank, Population and Human Resource Division.

———. 2002. *Indonesia Health Strategy in a Post-Crisis, Decentralizing Indonesia.* Report No. 29298-IND. Washington, DC: World Bank.

———. 2005. *Decentralization, Service Delivery and Governance in Indonesia: Findings from the Governance and Decentralization Survey (GDS).* Jakarta: World Bank.

———. 2008. *Investing in Indonesia's Health: Challenges and Opportunities for Future Public Spending. Health Public Expenditure Review 2008.* Jakarta: World Bank.

———. 2009a. *Giving More Weight to Health: Assessing Fiscal Space for Health in Indonesia.* Jakarta: World Bank.

———. 2009b. *Indonesia's Doctors, Midwives, and Nurses: Current Stock, Increasing Needs, Future Challenges and Options.* Jakarta: World Bank.

CHAPTER 2

Indonesia's Health System and Policies Affecting the Health Workforce

With a population of almost 230 million, Indonesia is the fourth most populous country in the world. It is a low-middle-income country with a per capita gross national income (GNI) of US$1,650 and a national poverty rate of 16.7 percent (World Bank 2009c). A rapidly growing share of Indonesians, 30 percent in 2005, live in urban areas, and of those, the majority reside on Java (BPS 2008). Although the majority of Indonesians live in rural areas, conditions vary substantially between peri-urban rural and more remote areas, particularly in the eastern provinces. Indonesia's territory is made up of roughly 17,000 islands, of which about 7,000 are inhabited, adding to the country's geographic diversity.

Health Outcomes and the Health Workforce

Indonesia has made impressive gains in extending the reach of health services, especially primary care, over the past three decades. Since the 1970s, the government of Indonesia has constructed more than 8,000 health centers, or *puskesmas*, 22,000 auxiliary health centers, or *pustu*, and more than 450 public hospitals. As of 2005, these public facilities alone employed about 415,000 people. Approximately 6 percent of all Indonesian civil servants are health workers employed in the public sector.[1] The private health sector grew even faster during the period, in part as a result of government policies allowing public sector staff members to work part-time as private providers, a practice generally referred to as Indonesia's "legal dual practice."

In international comparisons, however, Indonesia's ratios of physicians and health workers, as well as hospital beds, to population are low (figure 2.1). The number of hospital beds per 1,000 population is one of the lowest in the East Asia and Pacific region, lower even than those of countries with much lower income, such as the Lao People's Democratic Republic and Vietnam. On a global scale, Indonesia has significantly fewer beds than other countries of a similar income level.

The increased supply of health care and the focus on primary care over the past few decades have contributed to significant improvements in some health outcomes, such as life expectancy and child mortality. Life expectancy at birth increased from 60 years in 1986 to 69 years in 2007, and the infant mortality rate (IMR) decreased from around 110 per 1,000 live births in the early 1980s to 34 per 1,000 live births in 2007 (BPS et al. 2008). Indonesia is on track to attain the Millennium Development Goal for child mortality (*Bappenas* 2009). According to global comparisons, Indonesia's IMR in 2006 was lower than the average for its income level, and its life expectancy was about average for its income (figure 2.2).

Indonesia's performance with regard to some other key health outcomes, however, including maternal mortality and child malnutrition, has been poor. Indonesia's maternal mortality ratio (MMR) is among the highest in the region and is much higher than one would expect for its income level. Furthermore, the prevalence of child malnutrition remains high (averaging 23 percent over the period 2000–06) and is high even in relation to its income level (figure 2.3) (World Bank 2008). Despite the significant improvements in life expectancy, under–age 5 mortality, and infant mortality, rates are worse than those in peer countries in the region, including China, Malaysia, the Philippines, Thailand, and Vietnam (table 2.1).

National average health indicators mask significant geographic and income-related disparities within the country. Indonesia is a large, diverse, and geographically dispersed country. In poorer provinces, such as Gorontalo and West Nusa Tenggara, infant and child mortality rates are four to five times those in richer provinces, such as Bali and Yogyakarta (World Bank 2008). In addition, health indicators for the poor are far worse than those for the rich: the child mortality rate among the poorest quintile in 2003 was 3.5 times the rate among the richest quintiles (figure 2.4) (*Bappenas* 2009).

Figure 2.1   Global Comparisons of Physician, Health Worker, and Hospital Bed Supply to Income

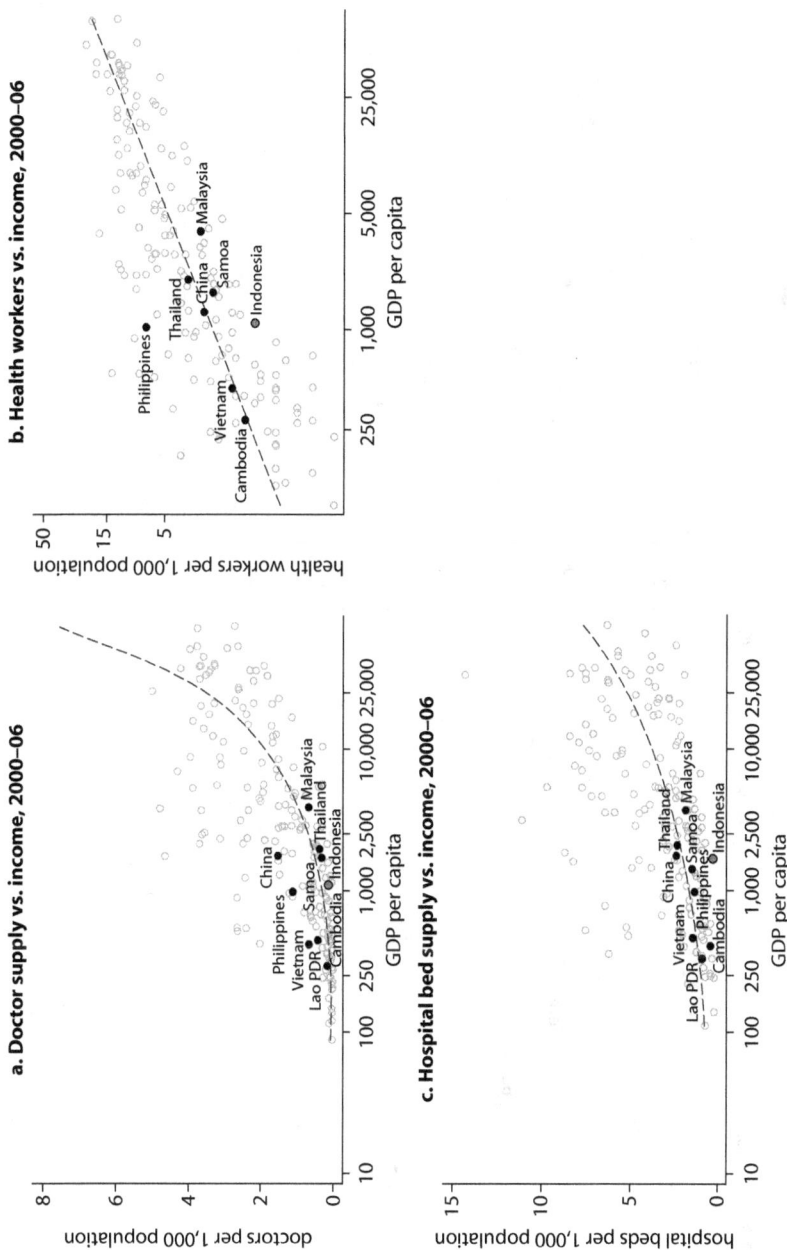

a. Doctor supply vs. income, 2000–06

b. Health workers vs. income, 2000–06

c. Hospital bed supply vs. income, 2000–06

Sources: WHO 2006; World Bank 2009c.

Note: GDP = gross domestic product. GDP data in current US$. Log scale. Doctor and GDP are data for latest available year.

Figure 2.2   Life Expectancy and Infant Mortality versus Income, 2006

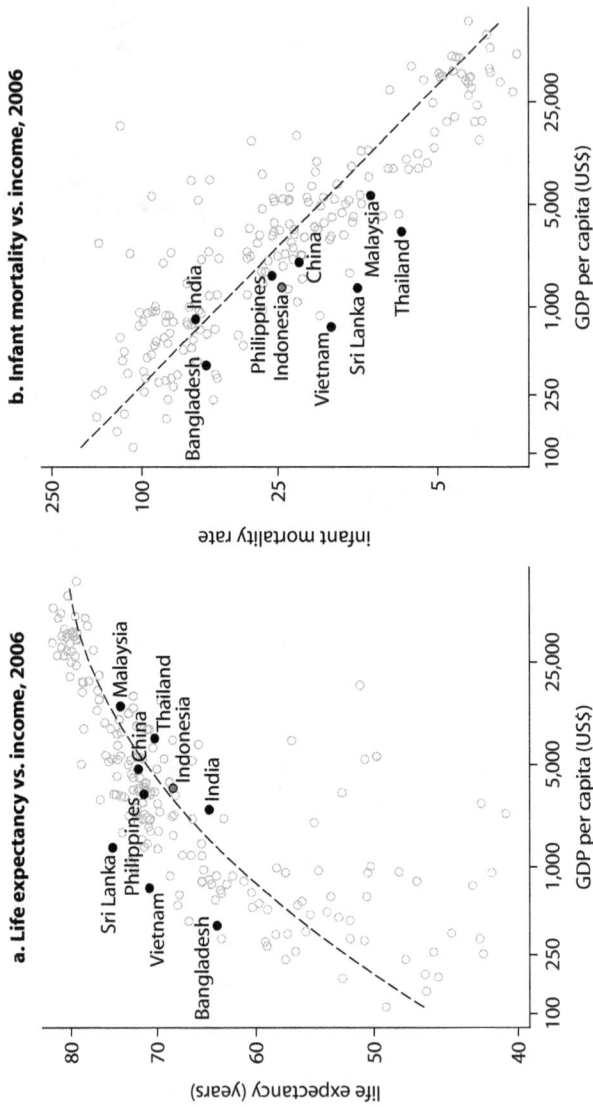

a. Life expectancy vs. income, 2006

b. Infant mortality vs. income, 2006

Source: World Bank 2009c.

Note: GDP = gross domestic product. Log scale.

Figure 2.3 Maternal Mortality and Child Nutrition versus Income, 2000–06

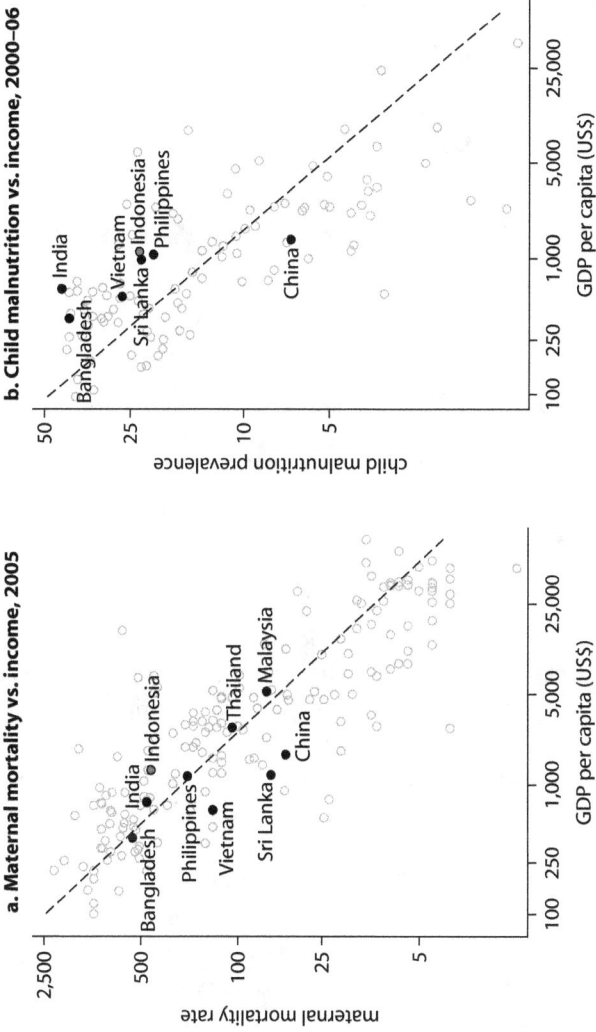

a. Maternal mortality vs. income, 2005

b. Child malnutrition vs. income, 2000–06

Source: World Bank 2009c.
Note: GDP = gross domestic product. Log scale.

Table 2.1   Health Outcomes in Indonesia and Selected Countries, 2006

Country or region	Life expectancy	Under-5 mortality rate per 1,000 births	Infant mortality rate per 1,000 births	Maternal mortality ratio per 100,000 population (2005)	Child malnutrition rate (2000–06; %)
Bangladesh	64	69	52	570	41
China	72	24	20	45	7
India	64	76	57	450	44
Indonesia	68	34	26	420	23
Malaysia	74	12	10	62	—
Philippines	71	32	24	230	21
Sri Lanka	75	13	11	58	23
Thailand	70	8	7	110	—
Vietnam	71	17	15	150	27
East Asia and Pacific (EAP)	67	44	35	286	24
Lower-middle-income countries (LMC)	68	45	34	233	11

Source: World Bank 2009c.

Note: — = not available. EAP and LMC numbers are unweighted country averages.

The mixed performance of Indonesia's health system suggests that Indonesia faces equity and quality of care challenges that go beyond increasing the supply of health care. Increased supply of health services does not necessarily equate to improved accessibility or utilization. For example, outpatient utilization rates at both public and private facilities remain lower than they were before the 1997–98 financial crisis hit Indonesia, when utilization rates declined by 30 percent. Almost one-half of those reporting illness rely on self-treatment in Indonesia.

Once people seek treatment at a facility, the quality of services they receive is often poor, as indicated by analyses using 1997 Indonesia Family Life Survey (IFLS)[2] data to study the quality of care providers (Barber, Gertler, and Harimurti 2007a). This report follows up on issues related to provider quality by updating the 1997 analysis with information from the latest round of the IFLS. In addition to low-quality services, health workers, in particular physicians, are often absent from public health facilities (Chaudhury et al. 2006), and large inequities exist in the distribution of health workers among the different regions in Indonesia.

Figure 2.4   Inequalities among Provinces in Infant and Child Mortality in Indonesia, 2007

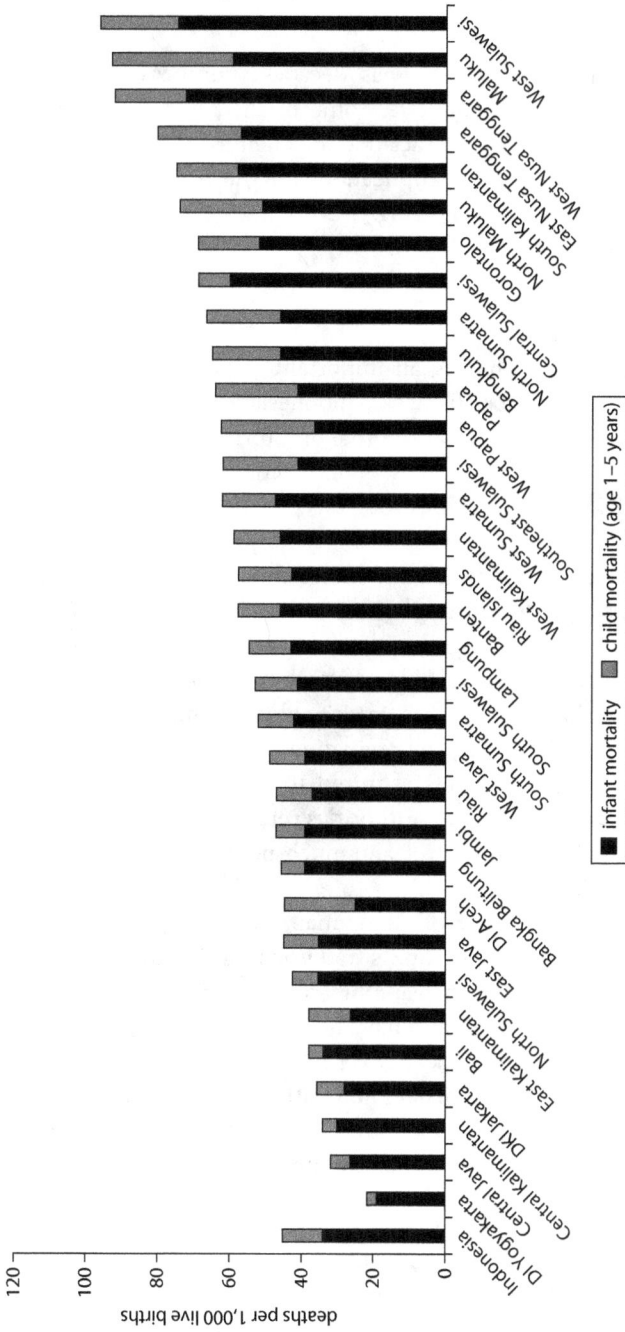

Source: BPS et al. 2008.

Policies Affecting the Supply and Quality of the Health Workforce

As mentioned above, over the past decades a number of important reforms have taken place in Indonesia. Some of the reforms are specific to the health sector, such as contract doctor schemes, and others are not sector specific but have serious implications for the health sector, for example, decentralization. The following is a brief review of the most important reforms and transitions.

Decentralization

Decentralization is having an important impact on the performance of the health workforce. In 2000, Indonesia started a new era in which decentralization plays a central role in efforts to improve the responsiveness of services to the needs of local communities. The "big bang" of decentralization in Indonesia took place in 2001 and was accompanied by profound changes in the responsibility for provision of services and in the ways that human, financial, and material resources are managed.

Responsibility for the implementation of health services was transferred to local governments, together with almost a quarter-million health workers. It was not a physical relocation, only an administrative one. Under decentralization, districts are responsible for employment, deployment, and payments. However, the regulations that delegate authority to make decisions and the budgets required to implement them are vague. In reality, central government authorities retain key decision-making responsibilities and financial control, and much-needed civil service reforms have not materialized.

As a result of the lack of skilled manpower in many districts, as well as its own reluctance to give up its traditional duties, the Ministry of Health is still deeply involved in planning and managing regional staff and programs. Existing sectoral laws have not been amended, adding to the confusion over the role of local governments. The development of sectoral objectives, policies, and plans, and related tasks, such as setting minimum performance standards, manpower planning, and preparation of the annual *formasi* exercise,[3] are still done centrally by the ministry (World Bank 2005).

Law No. 32/2004 was enacted with the purpose of addressing uncertainties and irregularities of the first decentralization law, Law No. 22/1999. The process of producing regulations to implement the law took a long time, and although PP No. 38/2008 (*Peraturan Pemerintah*, or government regulation) provides some details on the division of responsibilities between administrative levels, it remains too general.

Deployment Policies

In the late 1960s and 1970s, Indonesia's health system development was based on health centers at subdistrict and district-level hospitals (MoH 1982), with the main goal of providing access to primary care. The number of public health facilities grew steadily. Community services were included as well, staffed by doctors, midwives, and nurses under civil service contracts. To ensure adequate coverage in remote or very remote areas, it was made mandatory for civil servant staff members to serve a certain period of time in public facilities in a location determined by the government.

Until the early 1990s, all medical school graduates automatically became civil servants and were obliged to serve two to five years at a *puskesmas*. The term would be five years if the *puskesmas* was considered to be in a regular or more urbanized area, three years in a rural area, and two years in a more remote area. After serving in a remote area, physicians were also more likely to be accepted for further specialist training through the public system. As a result, by the 1980s, Indonesia's health system was close to providing universal coverage for primary and basic care, and essentially all doctors, midwives, and nurses were employed as civil servants. The private health care sector at the time was limited.

In response to the fiscal crisis of the late 1980s, however, the government in the early 1990s introduced an overall policy of zero growth of the civil service, as a measure to control public spending. Unlike other countries that introduced such measures, Indonesia provided no exception for medical doctors. This policy had a strong impact, reducing the number of health workers in the public sector, especially physicians,[4] as it eliminated the main incentive for deployment to remote areas. A relatively short period of mandatory service would now be followed by appointment to a civil service position.

To mitigate the effect of this change, the Ministry of Health initiated the *Pegawai Tidak Tetap* (PTT), or contract physician scheme, that hired recent medical school graduates as contractors, not as civil servants, and required a period of service in underserved areas. After their first three years, PTT doctors had the opportunity to continue their education, go into the private sector, or become civil servants by taking the national civil service examination. Those PTT doctors who had served in remote or very remote areas through the PTT scheme would generally receive priority in the subsequent civil service recruitment process. At the same time, changes were made to the village midwife program, which also started recruiting midwives under PTT contract schemes, with the expectation that the midwives would establish themselves as private providers after a number of years as contractors.

The PTT policy changed over time,[5] and in early 2000 the number of graduates directly recruited into the civil service began to fall. If one assumes that about 5,000 medical students graduate each year (World Bank 2009b), the public sector only absorbed about 40 percent through the PTT program. Medical graduates were growing more dissatisfied with the program policy and mandatory service. As a result, in 2007, compulsory PTT contracts were abolished.

The government remained concerned about providing medical care in remote and rural areas, however. A new policy was established offering a six-month period of service in remote areas for new graduates and an attractive salary package. In addition to the base salary, the new graduates received a monthly bonus amounting to as much as two-and-a-half times the base for very remote postings. This incentive package (generous remuneration and a short term of service), combined with a growing number of medical graduates entering the labor market after an expansion in the number of medical schools, has increased the interest of graduates in rural and remote postings. In addition, service as a PTT contract doctor in a remote area still contributes to positive evaluation for recruitment into the civil service.

Planning for Health Workforce Needs

Since the 1980s, the Ministry of Health has used several approaches to determine staff needs, using projections based on community health status, demographic changes, and existing health programs. The earliest approach was to use minimum standards for staffing needs, for example, one doctor per *puskesmas*. This was widely considered impractical because it did not reflect actual need. Although guidelines for new methods that take account of demand have been distributed, little is known about local governments' actual use of them (World Bank 2008).

After the 2001 decentralization, districts received authority to manage *puskesmas* and public hospitals, but the authority to hire and fire staff remains vague. The districts direct requests for new staff, particularly strategic staff such as doctors, midwives, and nurses, to the Ministry of Health through the province. Most districts still refer to national staffing standards rather than actual demand for services when sending their staffing request.

The Ministry of Health allocates staff based on available resources and on the *formasi* for a particular district, although available *formasi* do not always match with district need. The licensing of new private health providers and service points is the responsibility of local governments. However, no clear guidelines or criteria exist as to how to determine the need for new establishments. After decentralization, the central-level planning unit lost much of its information on the number of private providers.

Dual Practice and Provider Payment Methods

The policy of allowing public employees to work as private providers was intended to create an incentive for physicians and midwives to stay longer in their duty posts. However, small numbers of patients, lack of access to further education, and missed opportunities are common in remote areas and often still make it difficult to retain personnel. The village midwife program has been successful in deploying midwives to villages, but it also suffers from high turnover, low motivation, and retention problems.

Provider payment methods are among many tools policy makers can use to improve efficiency and are one of the critical factors affecting health workforce behavior.[6] In Indonesia, only a very few purchasing and payment methods are used, for example, salaries for civil servants and PTT contractors in public primary care, and fees for services in hospitals and those of private providers. These methods do not sufficiently link performance to payment, nor do they create incentives to provide better-quality services.

Public Expenditures

Indonesia's public expenditures in the health sector increased significantly over the past decade (*Bappenas* 2009) but remain low compared to those of other countries in the region (Rokx et al. 2009; World Bank 2008). Increases in health spending reflect the government's priority on health, relative to other sectors, as well as the availability of fiscal space. Indonesia's capacity to increase health spending grows as fiscal space increases, even with the current financial crisis.

Fiscal space implies not only an increase in nominal spending, but also improving the efficiency of current outlays (World Bank 2009a). The wages of the health workforce compose the largest share of public spending on health—81 percent of local government routine health expenditures (World Bank 2008). Using various payment allowances more strategically and implementing results-based payment mechanisms are important considerations in financing both more and better-quality health services (Vujicic, Ohiri, and Sparkes 2009).

The Quality of Educational Institutions

The health education system itself, the accreditation of education institutions, and the certification of health workers are subjects of concern over quality. Although some systems have been established, such as that which accredits medical, midwifery, and nursing schools, accreditation is not performed by an independent body. In addition, serious deficiencies exist in the standards, making accreditation very difficult to begin with, and accreditations that have been conducted are not publicized. At the same time, private institutions producing large numbers of physicians, midwives, and nurses are growing rapidly with little oversight over their quality (World Bank 2009b).

Growth of the Private Sector

Although the private health sector has grown in scale, oversight by the public sector remains very limited. Little is known about private providers, the quality of their services, and how many hours they work. The government has lost most of its ability to influence and oversee the private sector, the quality and provision of its services, and its geographic distribution. Some recent studies do address the private sector and will be discussed where relevant, including the Initiative for Maternal Mortality Programme Assessment (IMMPACT) studies, which focus on midwives, and a recent study on health workers on Java.

Estimates for all categories of health care providers indicate a growing private sector health workforce (see Knowles and Marzolf 2003). These providers work in private facilities (private hospitals, treatment clinics) or in their own private practices, with or without an appointment by the government. Moreover, because the membership lists and associated information that the professional societies maintain are not up to date (Heywood and Harahap 2009), it is likely that many of the studies significantly underestimate the size of the private sector.

Underlying Transitions

In Indonesia, as in many other countries, fertility rates have declined and the population is starting to age. This demographic transition and its associated epidemiological transition will change the composition of demand for health services and necessitate additional reforms to health workforce planning and management. A number of events in the future may put additional stress on the health sector and human resources in particular. The changing disease patterns (rapidly emerging noncommunicable diseases [NCDs] and injuries, while communicable diseases continue to spread) and reemerging health issues such as polio, HIV/AIDS, and avian influenza are likely to require a different skill mix.

More people will suffer from NCDs as a result of aging and increased prevalence of risk factors such as obesity and smoking.[7] The demand for curative and inpatient care will increase, with important implications for the number of hospital beds required, as well as skill requirements for new health personnel. At the same time, the demand for core public health functions (surveillance, immunization, health promotion) will continue or increase.

In the meantime, health service delivery in Indonesia relies on a one-size-fits-all model, although great variation exists in health needs across Indonesia's vast and diverse territory. Varied health outcomes reflecting performance are seen, with rapidly declining infant mortality and maternal mortality rates in provinces such as Java and Bali, but to a far less extent in eastern Indonesia, for example. The health sector will need to respond to this variation in demand with changes in its staffing policies and staff skill mix.

Notes

1. Based on data from the national civil service agency, BKN *(Badan Kepegawaian Negara)*, for 2003; http://www.bkn.go.id/stat_indo.

2. The IFLS is a data source available at http://www.rand.org/labor/FLS/IFLS.

3. The *formasi* is an annual update of authorized civil service (*Pegawai Negeri*, or PNS) posts in central agencies and regional governments. Local governments recruit based on the *formasi*, under strict guidelines and supervision by the Ministry of State Apparatus Reform (MENPAN).

4. The trends in density of health workers for population show an increase from 1985 to 1992, but a decrease after 1992, when the zero-growth policy was enacted and no new medical personnel could be recruited (Barber, Gertler, and Harimurti 2007b). The PTT program, however, helped to reverse the negative impact, and there has been an increase in ratios since its inception.

5. For a detailed overview of the PTT program over the past two decades, see Kluyskens and Firdaus (2007) and Ruswendi (2007).

6. "Provider payment" refers to processes through which funds are transferred from purchasers to the providers for health services (Gottret, Schieber, and Waters 2008).

7. These changes and the subsequent change in demand for health care were estimated in a recent study for the provinces of East Java and Central Java. According to the estimates, the relative importance of NCDs in the future disease burden in these two provinces will increase from 39 percent in 2005 to 56 percent in 2020, if the assumption of significant reductions in communicable diseases holds. Even holding communicable diseases equal, the NCD share would rise to 43 percent (Choi et al. 2007).

References

Bappenas. 2009. *Pembangunan Kesehatan dan Gizi di Indonesia: Overview dan Arah ke Depan: Background Study RPJMN 2010–2014* (Health and Nutritional Development in Indonesia: An Overview and Future Directions: Background Study RPJMN 2010–2014). Jakarta: *Bappenas*.

Barber, S. L., P. J. Gertler, and P. Harimurti. 2007a. "Differences in Access to High-Quality Outpatient Care in Indonesia." *Health Affairs* 26 (3): w352–66.

———. 2007b. "The Contribution of Human Resources for Health to the Quality of Care in Indonesia." *Health Affairs* 26 (3): w367–79.

BPS (*Badan Pusat Statistik* [Indonesia Statistics Bureau]), National Family Planning Coordinating Board, Ministry of Health, and Macro International. 2008. *Demographic and Health Survey 2007.* Calverton, MD: BPS and Macro International. http://demografi.bps.go.id/versi2/index.php.

Chaudhury, N., J. Hammer, M. Kremer, K. Muralidharn, and F. H. Rogers. 2006. "Missing in Action: Teacher and Health Worker Absence in Developing Countries." *Journal of Economic Perspectives* 20 (1): 91–116.

Choi, Y., J. Friedman, P. Heywood, and S. Kosen. 2007. "Forecasting Health Care Demand in a Middle-Income Country: Disease Transitions in East and Central Java, Indonesia." Research Working Paper. World Bank, Washington, DC.

Gottret, P., G. J. Schieber, and H. R. Waters, eds. 2008. *Good Practices in Health Financing: Lessons from Reforms in Low- and Middle-Income Countries.* Washington, DC: World Bank.

Heywood, P. F., and N. P. Harahap. 2009. "Human Resources for Health at the District Level in Indonesia: The Smoke and Mirrors of Decentralization." *Human Resources for Health 2009* 7:6.

Kluyskens, J., and M. Firdaus. 2007. " Assessment of Regulatory Responsibilities and Management of Health Work Force." Consultant report, World Bank, Jakarta.

Knowles, J. C., and J. R. Marzolf. 2003. *Health Financing for the Poor in Indonesia.* Consultant Report. Jakarta: World Bank.

MoH (Ministry of Health). 1982. *National Health System.* Jakarta: Indonesia.

Rokx, C., G. Schieber, P. Harimurti, A. Tandon, and A. Somanathan. 2009. *Health Financing in Indonesia: A Reform Road Map*. Washington, DC: World Bank.

Ruswendi, D. 2007. *Evaluation Study of the Deployment Policy for Contract (PTT) Doctors/Dentists in Remote Areas in 4 HWS Project Provinces: Kalimantan Barat; Kalimantan Timur; Sumatra Barat; Jambi. Year 2006–2007*. ADB Consultant Report. Manila: Asian Development Bank.

Vujicic, M., K. Ohiri, and S. Sparkes. 2009. *Working in Health: Financing and Managing the Public Sector Health Workforce*. Washington, DC: World Bank.

WHO (World Health Organization). 2006. *Working Together for Health: The World Health Report 2006*. Geneva: WHO.

World Bank. 2005. *Civil Service Reforms at the Regional Level: Opportunities and Constraints*. Jakarta: World Bank.

———. 2008. *Investing in Indonesia's Health: Challenges and Opportunities for Future Public Spending. Health Public Expenditure Review 2008*. Jakarta: World Bank.

———. 2009a. *Giving More Weight to Health: Assessing Fiscal Space for Health in Indonesia*. Jakarta: World Bank.

———. 2009b. *Indonesia's Doctors, Midwives, and Nurses: Current Stock, Increasing Needs, Future Challenges, and Options*. Jakarta: World Bank.

———. 2009c. *World Development Indicators*. Washington, DC: World Bank.

CHAPTER 3

The Supply and Distribution of Health Practitioners and Health Facilities

The current Indonesian health system comprises public and private health services. The provision of public health services is the responsibility of the Ministry of Health (MoH) and subnational governments. These public sector actors deliver both inpatient and outpatient services. Meanwhile, private health care has been growing rapidly. It consists of ambulatory services provided by private practitioners and by government medical staff operating private practices part-time, as well as private clinics and specialized hospitals that provide inpatient care.

Indonesia's approach to health system development has followed the Alma Ata "Health for All" paradigm in that it has focused on integrated service provision at the primary care level.[1] *Puskesmas* are the linchpin of the health system, which is characterized by heavy reliance on health workers, not necessarily physicians, in the field. As with many developing countries at that time, Indonesia expanded its rural primary health facilities and moved away from sole attention to urban hospitals. Indonesia has largely achieved the goal of expanding its primary care infrastructure and placing a health worker in each village. In addition, by legalizing dual practice, the government has promoted increased availability of services as the private health sector has grown.

Changes in the Supply of Health Practitioners, 1996–2006

This section examines the growth in the number of physicians and midwives in Indonesia. Data on the number of nurses are not reliable, and therefore they are not included in the analysis of the supply of services. It is important to distinguish between public and private providers, although the distinction has been somewhat ambiguous since dual practice was allowed by law in the 1970s. Since then the government of Indonesia has allowed physicians and midwives to earn additional income from private practices operated after public working hours, which, if lucrative, could lead to improved retention of health workers in rural and remote areas. In addition to providing more earning opportunities for health workers, allowing dual practice was also expected to increase the supply of health services by creating an incentive for providers to work longer hours.

At present, almost 70 percent of *puskesmas* physicians and about 93 percent of midwives also provide private services during nonpublic hours (Ensor et al. 2008; Indonesia Family Life Survey [IFLS] 2007, http://www.rand.org/labor/FLS/IFLS). However, as has been the case in many countries where dual practice occurs, it may have induced provider preference for settlement in urban areas, where private practice opportunities are generally greater. For Indonesia, analysis of the Survey of Village Potential (*Potensi Desa*, or PODES) data provides some insight into the increased availability of private services.[2] This will be discussed below, after a more general discussion of growth in the numbers of different types of practitioners.

Indonesian Physicians

PODES data indicate that Indonesia has more than 18 physicians for every 100,000 people, a 6 percent increase in the ratio since 1996 (table 3.1).[3] Although the ratio rose from 15.7 physicians per 100,000 people in 1996, to 18.4 in 2006, it remains low by international standards (World Bank 2009). Moreover, one should note that right after the financial crisis, the number of physicians per 100,000 people decreased substantially, particularly in the wake of the zero growth policy for the civil service that was subsequently put in place (Barber, Gertler, and Harimurti 2007b). That should be kept in mind when interpreting the seemingly small increase in the health worker to population ratio over the past 10 years.

The aggregate numbers mask significant disparities in the number of health workers between urban and rural areas, with a clear urban bias. Although almost 70 percent of Indonesians lived in rural areas in 2005,[4] urban areas in all regions consistently have more physicians per 100,000

Table 3.1   Distribution of Physicians in Indonesia, 1996–2006

	Number			Per 100,000 residents		
Area	1996	2006	Change (%)	1996	2006	Change (%)
National	31,543	39,684	25.8	15.65	18.36	17.4
Urban	23,879	32,083	34.4	40.24	36.18	−10.1
Rural	7,664	7,601	−0.82	5.39	5.96	10.6
Java and Bali	19,635	23,944	22.0	16.18	18.53	14.5
Urban	16,141	20,896	29.5	38.97	34.06	−12.6
Rural	3,494	3,048	−12.8	4.37	4.49	2.8
Sumatra	6,208	8,531	37.4	14.62	18.72	28.1
Urban	4,326	6,203	43.4	41.98	41.16	−1.9
Rural	1,882	2,328	23.7	5.85	7.63	30.4
Other Provinces	5,700	7,209	26.5	15.09	17.44	15.6
Urban	3,412	4,984	46.1	44.76	40.63	−9.2
Rural	2,288	2,225	−2.8	7.59	7.66	0.9

Source: PODES (Potensi Desa) survey from Indonesia's Central Bureau of Statistics (BPS) 1996, 2006, http://www.rand.org/labor/bps/podes/.

people, with ratios at least six times greater than those in rural areas. In 2007, urban areas had 36 physicians for every 100,000 people, whereas rural areas had only 6 for every 100,000 people. Only 20 percent of physicians are based in rural areas where the majority of the population lives. The gap between urban and rural remains very large despite some significant proportional improvements since 1996, when the difference was even larger, at eight times greater in urban areas.

The disparities in availability of health providers may be even more pronounced among urban, rural, remote, and very remote regions. Some data caveats to keep in mind when interpreting these results are the changes introduced in the classifications of rural, remote, and urban areas, as well as changes in geographical boundaries of villages since decentralization (that is, the merging of villages and the reassignment of some to different districts). The definition of "rural" used in data sources is also broad and may take in a very heterogeneous group of settlements, ranging from very remote, isolated hamlets to periurban areas. Although, in absolute terms, fewer physicians were practicing in rural areas in 2007 than in 1997, the physician to population ratio increased by 10 percent. This phenomenon is due in part to emigration from rural areas, which has reduced rural population density.

A regional analysis shows further that disparities between urban and rural areas are even greater in provinces outside of Java and Bali.[5] Where Java and Bali follow the trend in the national average, Sumatra and Other

Provinces have even greater disparities between urban and rural areas in the ratio of physicians to population.

Changes in contract physician (pegawai tidak tetap, or PTT) program policy over recent years (see chapter 2) are reflected in the fluctuating numbers of PTT contract doctors (table 3.2). Whereas almost 3,000 new graduates entered the health labor force as PTT doctors during the first decade of the program, fewer entered when dissatisfaction with the program became widespread. After the program ceased to be compulsory, the numbers declined further. The subsequent introduction of a six-month contract, with a high salary for remote area service, appears to have increased the number of graduates signing up. At the same time, the high level of turnover that is institutionalized by offering terms as short as six months can also result in a temporary lack of physicians and may also impair quality, since most recent graduates only have limited practical experience.

The relatively large decline in the number of PTT physicians in *puskesmas* in areas rated "ordinary" (neither "remote" nor "very remote") could indicate that more graduates have recently moved into private practice. Moreover, the dual practice policy may have further encouraged new graduates to go into private practice and seek employment in more urban areas. In rural areas, fewer opportunities arise to gain extra income from private practice, making rural, and especially remote, postings unattractive. Earlier research in Indonesia and elsewhere has demonstrated that the bonus in addition to base salary that must be paid to attract physicians to work in remote areas can be prohibitively costly (Chomitz et al. 1998). However the bonus for PTT doctors to serve in very remote areas, together with the limited service period, has attracted a rising number of new graduates.

Table 3.2   PTT Physicians Recruitment and Location Classification, 1992–2007

Period	PTT doctors recruitment and location classification			
	Ordinary	Remote	Very remote	Total
1992–2002	19,549	7,042	3,270	29,861
Average per year	1,955	704	327	2,986
2003–06	3,826	2,517	1,885	8,228
Average per year	957	629	471	2,057
2006–07	995	1,489	1,700	4,184
Average per year	498	745	850	2,093

Source: Ruswendi 2007.

Indonesian Midwives

Indonesia has no central registration system for nurses or midwives, and hence no up-to-date information is available on their numbers. According to PODES, which at present is the most accurate source of data, Indonesia had almost 80,000 midwives in 2006. The number of midwives per capita increased from 35 per 100,000 population in 1996, to 37 per 100,000 in 2006. As with physicians, this aggregate figure masks imbalances in distribution. Unlike the distribution of physicians, however, rural areas have higher ratios than urban areas (table 3.3). The PODES data also show that ratios are higher in provinces outside Java and Bali and in the poorer provinces of eastern and central Indonesia, indicating a more equal distribution of midwives.

The national ratio of midwives to population has changed only marginally over time in urban areas. Urbanization has increased, and more midwives are residing in urban areas. Different patterns emerge when one analyzes changes in the numbers and ratios for different regions. The total number of midwives in Java and Bali did not change over time, but a shift took place between urban and rural areas. Rural areas had almost 30 midwives per 100,000 population in 1996, but only 27 per 100,000 in 2006. In 2006, urban areas had more midwives, 25 per 100,000 population, than they had in 1996.

In Other Provinces, the ratio of midwives increased over the decade from 39 to almost 52 per 100,000 population. A 40 percent increase in the absolute number of midwives in rural areas contributed to this change, with

Table 3.3   Distribution of Midwives in Indonesia, 1996 and 2006

Region	Level			Per 100,000 residents		
	1996	2006	Change (%)	1996	2006	Change (%)
National	71,015	79,661	12.17	35.22	36.86	4.64
Urban	17,958	27,809	54.86	30.26	31.36	3.63
Rural	47,049	51,852	10.21	37.29	40.69	9.12
Java and Bali	33,436	33,755	0.95	27.55	26.12	−5.19
Urban	9,874	15,388	55.84	23.84	25.08	5.21
Rural	23,562	18,367	−22.05	29.47	27.06	−8.19
Sumatra	22,823	24,645	7.98	53.73	54.09	0.67
Urban	4,787	7,241	51.26	46.45	48.05	3.45
Rural	18,036	17,404	−3.50	56.06	57.07	1.80
Other Provinces	14,756	21,261	44.08	39.07	51.45	31.67
Urban	3,297	5,180	57.11	43.25	42.23	−2.36
Rural	11,459	16,081	40.34	38.02	55.34	45.55

Source: PODES 1996, 2006.

the ratio of midwives to population also showing an increase. These shifts may be explained by the strong emphasis of the government on placing midwives in rural areas through the village midwife program, *Bidan di Desa* (BDD),which was started in 1992.

The main focus of the BDD program initially was to place midwives in rural villages under three-year contracts. After the initial three years, midwives could renew their contract for another three years, but that was the maximum period. Midwives were expected to have created a sufficiently large client base by then to stay employed through the provision of private services. Alternatively, the district health office could employ the midwives under regional PTT contracts. Even during their contract years, the midwives were permitted to have a private practice, which often doubled their income. Midwives in remote and very remote areas also received a considerable bonus on top of their salaries, which could be provided by both the central and local governments.

With the introduction of the *Desa Siaga*, or "alert village," program in 2008, village midwives remain contract employees and have the option to become civil servants after their contract period.[6] Although it is known that many have the desire to enter the civil service eventually because of employment stability and other financial advantages, little information is available on how many midwives actually enter the civil service through this program.

Indonesian Nurses

PODES data show a decrease of nearly 50 percent in the number of nurses between 1996 and 2006, even though an estimated 34,000 new nurses enter the labor market each year.[7] It is very unlikely that none of these new entrants are recorded in the PODES survey. PODES estimates may be biased downward because nurses do not run their own practices (at least legally), and so village heads may underestimate the number of nurses in the community. Indonesia Health Profiles, published by the Ministry of Health (MoH 2007a), and the GDS-2 survey both suggest significantly higher numbers of nurses than PODES. Hence data on nurses are ambiguous at best, and therefore details on their numbers and distributions are not discussed in this work.

At the same time, Indonesian nurses fulfill an extremely important function in the health system and are often the only health workers in remote and poor rural areas. They are often required to carry out services and provide medical treatments that they are neither trained for nor allowed to perform under the medical practice law. Precisely because nurses provide a large part of health services in remote areas and to the poor, the dearth of data regarding nurses needs urgent attention. The need for better data on nurses' practices and their distribution, as well as on practitioner quality, is pressing (discussed in the next chapter).

Changes in Staffing at the Public Health Facilities, *Puskesmas* and *Pustu*, 1997–2007

The Indonesia Family Life Survey (IFLS) facility surveys show that physician numbers increased significantly, from 1.5 physicians per *puskesmas* in 1997 to 1.9 physicians per *puskesmas* in 2007 (table 3.4). Although the increase is similar in urban and rural areas, *puskesmas* in urban areas have, on average, more than 2.0 physicians, while they have only 1.6 in rural areas. A regional comparison shows that the increase was especially large in Sumatra and Other Provinces, 0.6 more physicians, on average, while in Java and Bali there were 0.3 more physicians per *puskesmas* in 2007. Despite these figures, which suggest that those areas are catching up, Java and Bali still have the highest number of physicians, on average, with close to 2.0 per *puskesmas* (table 3.5). Java and Bali remain the preferred region to serve in.

At the same time, however, the IFLS shows a doubling in the number of *puskesmas* without any physician in 2007, from 3.4 percent to 7 percent. In rural areas especially, almost 9 percent of *puskesmas* are without a physician. In Java and Bali and in Sumatra the share of *puskesmas* without physicians increased more than threefold, while in Other Provinces the number decreased. Nevertheless, despite the

Table 3.4   Average Facility Staffing of *Puskesmas* and *Pustu* in Urban and Rural Settings, 1997–2007

	National		Urban		Rural	
Facility	1997	2007	1997	2007	1997	2007
Puskesmas						
Number of physicians	1.51	1.90	1.63	2.04	1.29	1.58
No physician (%)	3.40	7.00	2.44	6.18	5.08	8.65
Number of midwives	5.85	3.69	4.99	3.78	7.30	3.51
Number of nurses	5.05	6.14	4.88	6.02	5.34	6.42
Pustu						
Number of midwives	0.98	0.81	1.14	1.06	0.84	0.50
Number of nurses	1.08	1.06	1.21	1.19	0.99	0.86

Source: IFLS 1997, 2007. http://www.rand.org/labor/FLS/IFLS.

Table 3.5   Average Facility Staffing of *Puskesmas* and *Pustu* by Region, 1997–2007

Facility	National		Java and Bali		Sumatra		Other Provinces	
	1997	2007	1997	2007	1997	2007	1997	2007
Puskesmas								
Number of physicians	1.51	1.90	1.68	1.96	1.19	1.85	1.09	1.62
No physician (%)	3.4	7.0	1.5	5.9	2.0	6.8	15.9	11.3
Number of midwives	5.85	3.69	5.76	3.44	6.33	5.28	5.62	3.18
Number of nurses	5.05	6.14	4.58	5.60	6.16	7.16	5.84	7.61
Pustu								
Number of midwives	0.98	0.81	1.06	0.76	1.13	1.17	0.44	0.21
Number of nurses	1.08	1.06	1.02	1.09	1.16	1.08	1.16	0.89

Source: IFLS 1997, 2007, http://www.rand.org/labor/FLS/IFLS.

decrease in the share of centers without a physician, Other Provinces still reported 11.3 percent of *puskesmas* without a physician and, overall, had the lowest average number of physicians per *puskesmas*.

An increase in the average number of physicians per *puskesmas* coupled with a simultaneous increase in the number of *puskesmas* without a physician might appear contradictory at first but can be explained by the clustering of physicians in certain areas. The large range around the average numbers can be used to illustrate this point. In urban areas the number of doctors per facility ranges from 0 to 14, with an average of 2, and in rural areas the number varies from 0 to 10, with an average of 1.6 physicians per *puskesmas*.

In fact, the increase in the average number of physicians per *puskesmas* may mask a worsening of the situation. More *puskesmas* have no physician, while physicians cluster in urban *puskesmas* because of the greater opportunities for dual practice. Possible other explanations for this phenomenon could include the previously mentioned changes in the government's deployment policy for physicians.

The overall decline in the number of PTT contract physicians recruited over the period 1996–2007 (table 3.2) suggests that most of the additional doctors recruited to work in a *puskesmas* were hired as civil servants. Because there is little incentive, other than the six-month program, for doctors to work in rural areas with fewer private practice opportunities, they cluster in urban areas. Doctors recruited as civil servants do not get the bonus that PTT doctors receive when practicing in remote areas. Therefore, recruitment of doctors as civil servants with the aim of improving deployment and distribution will not necessarily improve deployment to remote areas.

It is recommended that policy move instead toward incentive-based payment schemes for physicians. The recent changes in the PTT contract doctors program to provide additional incentives for remote area service confirm that this can work. At the same time, the fact that the new contract term is only six months might imply that its impact is only temporary and not necessarily sustainable as a means of reducing the shortages and high turnover in areas most in need of more physicians.

As explained above, physicians working in *puskesmas* often prefer employment in urban areas because of dual practice opportunities, and the data show that two-thirds of these physicians are engaged in dual practice. Table 3.6 illustrates the proportion of *puskesmas* physicians who also provide services in the private sector.[8] Although the proportion has declined since 1997, it remains very high, at 68 percent in 2007. While two-thirds of *puskesmas* physicians engage in dual practice, the IFLS sample does not allow any conclusions to be drawn about dual practice among physicians in general, nor are data available regarding the division of labor (number of hours worked in each sector) of public and private providers.

The IFLS sample shows a large decrease in the number of midwives employed in *puskesmas* and *pustu*. Far fewer midwives were based in *puskesmas* in 2007—3.7 per facility versus 5.9 in 1997 (table 3.4). The reverse is true of nurses, who numbered 6.1 per facility in 2007, compared with approximately 5.1 in 1997. The number of midwives and nurses in *pustu* has also declined; rural areas in particular had significantly

Table 3.6   Proportion of *Puskesmas* Physicians with Dual Practice, 1997 and 2007

| | Puskesmas *physicians with private practice (%)* | |
Region	1997	2007
All sample	76.57	67.96
Urban	75.05	66.61
Rural	78.78	70.66
Sumatra	81.48	68.06
Urban	82.65	62.61
Rural	80.22	76.32
Java and Bali	77.23	70.03
Urban	74.19	69.00
Rural	82.91	72.90
Other Provinces	68.52	61.02
Urban	69.33	60.44
Rural	67.82	61.63

Source: IFLS 1997, 2007, http://www.rand.org/labor/FLS/IFLS.

fewer midwives in 2007. The decrease in the number of midwives in *puskesmas* can be explained in part by the government policy giving priority to deployment of midwives to the villages instead of the *puskesmas*. While these *Bidan di Desa* midwives remain under the supervision of the *puskesmas*, they are not based in the facility. More midwives also work as private providers.

Changes in the Supply of Public Health Facilities, 1996–2007

An impressive expansion of public health system infrastructure began in the 1970s, and by 2006, Indonesia had established more than 8,000 health centers, or *puskesmas*, of which nearly 31 percent provide inpatient care (MoH 2007a). Each *puskesmas* serves about 23,000 people within a service area of 24 square kilometers (MoH 2007a). The supply of public primary health services has further improved with the establishment of roughly 22,200 auxiliary health centers (*puskesmas pembantu*, or *pustu*) and nearly 5,800 mobile health centers, *puskesmas keliling*, of which 508 are four-wheeled and approximately 700 are on boats (MoH 2007a).[9]

The numbers of public hospitals and hospital beds have grown slowly and have failed to keep pace with population growth. In 1990, 404 hospitals and 59,000 public beds made up the "main system"[10] of facilities directly administered by the Ministry of Health, plus those operated by provinces and districts (World Bank 2008, MoH 2007b).[11] In 2007, the numbers rose to 582 hospitals and about 77,221 beds. *Puskesmas* operate as referral points for district and provincial hospitals, as well as for specialized facilities and other private hospitals.

The slow expansion in public hospital and bed numbers has been partly offset by an increase in private hospitals. In 1990, Indonesia had 352 private hospitals with approximately 31,000 beds, and that increased to 451 private hospitals with 52,300 beds by 2007 (MoH 2007b). Largely as a result of private sector growth, the overall bed to population ratio increased slightly over the period. It is important to note, however, that many private hospitals provide more specialized forms of care, and it remains unclear whether the overall expansion has been in line with Indonesia's changing burden of disease or was linked to need. Moreover, considerable disparities may exist in access to the additional beds.

Examining health infrastructure by province provides a mixed picture of physical access to health care, with large differences in numbers of *puskesmas* and hospital beds per capita. On average, every 100,000 Indonesians are served by 3.5 *puskesmas*, and every million Indonesians by 5.6 hospitals, equating to 2.5 hospital beds per 10,000 people. Although the number of *puskesmas* is considered sufficient to meet the established standard of one *puskesmas* per 30,000 people, disparities exist within and across provinces, and the supply is not based on a needs assessment. Most remote areas have fewer than one *puskesmas* per 100,000 people, and some areas do not even have one hospital per million, or less than two hospital beds per 10,000 people (figure 3.1).

Indonesian Physicians Providing Private Health Services

When one examines the growth in the supply of private health services, it is apparent that the number of physicians working privately increased by almost 10,000 over the decade studied, from 19,967 in 1996, to 29,634 in 2006. This represents a 48 percent increase in the number of physicians providing private services (table 3.7) and a 38 percent increase in physicians per 100,000 population. As expected, the growth in the number of physicians providing private services has been greatest in urban areas, with a 56 percent increase in absolute numbers. Rural areas experienced an increase of 21 percent, with four physicians providing private services for every 100,000 people in 2006. Regional comparisons show similar trends for all provinces except Sumatra, where the ratio per 100,000 people decreased in urban areas while increasing in rural areas (table 3.7).

In rural areas in particular, significant gains were made in the supply of privately provided services between 1997 and 2007, both in terms of percentage change and in the ratio per 100,000 people. In absolute numbers, however, the changes were much smaller, and the disparity in distribution of private services between urban and rural areas remains. The urban-rural gap in private services is even greater than the gap in the number of physicians, which supports the argument that urban areas continue to attract more physicians, in part because of the possibility of opening lucrative private practices. Change in the length of mandatory PTT service—now demanding only six months' service in remote areas—may have helped to increase the numbers of rural physicians, at least temporarily.

Indonesian Midwives Providing Private Health Services

The number of private midwife practices grew substantially between 1996 and 2006 (table 3.8). The much greater growth in midwife practices, compared with the increase in the number of midwives, can be explained by dual private-public practice. In 2006, many more midwives practiced privately than did so in 1996. The change has been particularly significant in Java and Bali, where the number of midwife practices have more than

52

Figure 3.1 Number of *Puskesmas* and Ratio of *Puskesmas* and Hospitals to Population, by Province, 2007

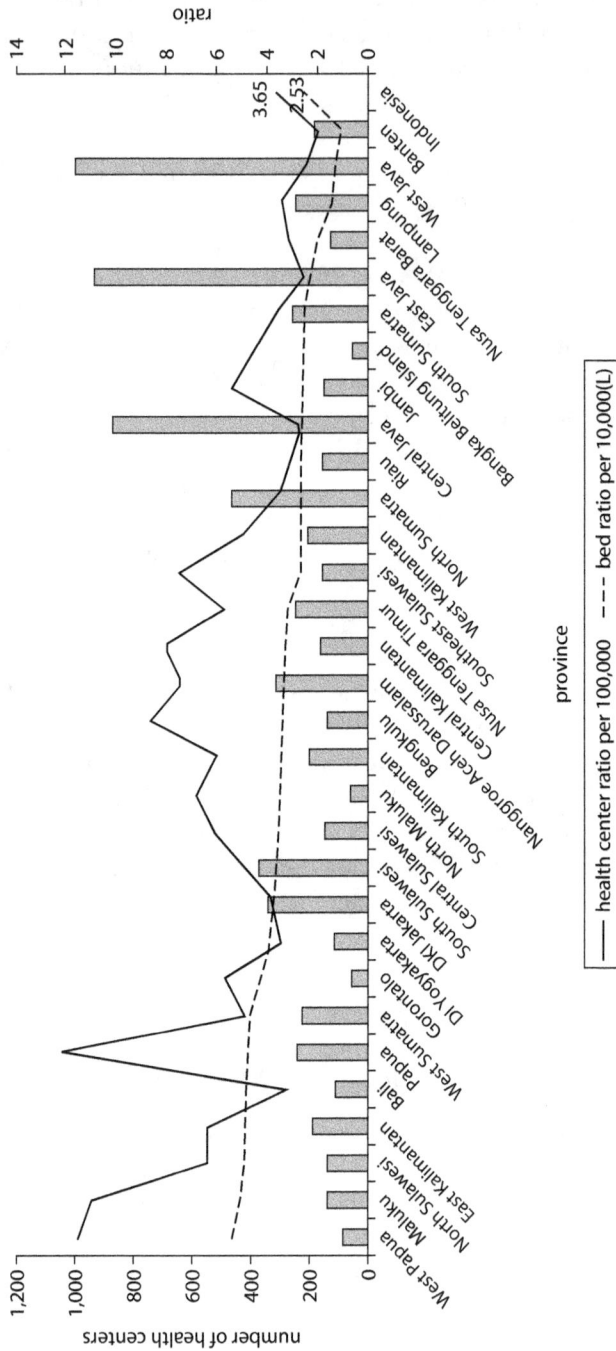

— health center ratio per 100,000   - - - bed ratio per 10,000(L)

Source: MoH 2007a.

Note: DI = *daerah istimewa*, or special region; DKI = *daerah khusus ibukota*, or special capital city district.

Table 3.7   Distribution of Physicians Providing Private Services in Indonesia, 1996–2006

	Level			Per 100,000 population		
Region	1996	2006	Change (%)	1996	2006	Change (%)
National	19,967	29,634	48.41	9.90	13.71	38.48
Urban	15,727	24,520	55.91	26.50	27.65	4.34
Rural	4,240	5,114	20.61	2.98	4.01	34.56
Java and Bali	13,332	19,950	49.64	10.98	15.44	40.62
Urban	10,762	17,213	59.94	25.98	28.06	8.01
Rural	2,570	2,737	6.50	3.21	4.03	25.55
Sumatra	3,888	5,425	39.53	9.15	11.91	30.16
Urban	2,940	4,007	36.29	28.53	26.59	−6.79
Rural	948	1,418	49.58	2.95	4.65	57.63
Other Provinces	2,747	4,259	55.04	7.27	10.31	41.82
Urban	2,025	3,300	62.96	26.57	26.90	1.24
Rural	722	959	32.83	2.40	3.30	37.50

Source: PODES (*Potensi Desa*) survey from Indonesia's Central Bureau of Statistics (BPS) 1996, 2006, http://www.rand.org/labor/bps/podes/.

Table 3.8   Distribution of Private Midwife Practices in Indonesia, 1996–2006

	Level			Per 100,000 population		
Region	1996	2006	Change (%)	1996	2006	Change (%)
National	17,278	44,616	158	8.57	20.64	140
Urban	988	18,684	1,791	1.66	21.07	1,169
Rural	16,290	25,932	59	11.45	20.34	77
Java and Bali	8,459	27,057	220	6.97	20.95	200
Urban	733	12,627	1,623	1.77	20.58	1,062
Rural	7,726	14,448	87	9.66	21.28	120
Sumatra	6,049	12,554	108	14.24	27.55	93
Urban	187	4,393	2,249	1.81	29.15	1,510
Rural	5,862	8,161	39	18.22	26.76	46
Other Provinces	2,770	4,987	80	7.33	12.07	64
Urban	68	1,664	2,347	0.86	13.56	1,476
Rural	2,702	3,323	22	8.96	11.43	27

Source: PODES (*Potensi Desa*) survey from Indonesia's Central Bureau of Statistics (BPS) 1996, 2006, http://www.rand.org/labor/bps/podes/.

tripled. In Sumatra the number doubled, and in Other Provinces it almost doubled. There continued to be more midwife practices in rural areas than urban areas in 2006, but the increase in the number of midwives in urban areas is still quite significant. This increase in urban areas may be explained by a preference for urban settlement by many midwives upon completion of their BDD contract.

It is also possible that the 1996 data capture the peak of the BDD program. By 2006, many of those midwives were likely to have moved back to urban areas when their contracts were not extended. In addition, after decentralization a rapid increase in new D3-level midwifery schools occurred, producing large numbers of midwives. The public sector could not absorb all new graduates, and as a result many went straight into private practice. As urban areas offer more job opportunities, the majority went or stayed there.

The attractiveness of the job may also play an important role in explaining the increase in the supply of midwives. Being a midwife and having a private practice is an attractive job opportunity for many women in Indonesia. A series of studies performed in two districts in West Java under the Initiative for Maternal Mortality Programme Assessment (IMMPACT) found that most midwives (93 percent) received income from private clinical practice and that on average, 58 percent of their total earnings came from private practice (Ensor et al. 2008).

One study, which sampled 207 midwives providing services in 227 villages, has shown that annual incomes for village midwives can be substantial. The mean private income of midwives in that study was US$2,508 per annum, and 10 percent had an annual income of more than US$11,000. Moreover, the IMMPACT study found that opportunities to generate additional income from private practice exist not only in urban areas but also in rural parts of Java. The fact that many young Indonesians are interested in working as midwives is reflected in the very high demand for midwifery education, as there are more than 600 midwifery schools in Indonesia.

Notes

1. The Alma Ata Conference was held in 1978 in Kazakhstan, which was a Soviet Republic at the time. The Alma Ata Declaration called for "urgent action by all governments, all health and development workers, and the world community to protect and promote the health of all people of the world" (WHO 1978).

2. The PODES (*Potensi Desa*, or Survey of Village Potential) survey from Indonesia's Central Bureau of Statistics (BPS); PODES data are accessed at http://www.rand.org/labor/bps/podes/.

3. Although the physicians registration database maintained by the Indonesian Medical Council (*Konsil Kedokteran Indonesia*, or KKI) is the most recent

and accurate database on the number of physicians, KKI data are only available for 2007 and do not include information about whether physicians are providing public, private, or dual practices. Therefore, in this book, PODES data are used. For more details on data and data sources, see World Bank 2009. The difference in the total physician numbers counted by KKI and PODES can be explained by the fact that PODES does not include doctors who work only in hospitals and secondary care or nonpracticing physicians, while KKI registration includes all doctors.

4. According to BPS and *Bappenas* data sources; this percentage is changing rapidly with ongoing urbanization.

5. The Java and Bali region includes Banten, West Java, Central Java, Yogyakarta, East Java, and Bali. Sumatra includes Sumatra (all), Riau, Jambi, Bengkulu, Lampung, and Bangka Belitung. Other Provinces includes Nusa Tenggara Timur (NTT), Nusa Tenggara Barat (NTB), Aceh, Kalimantan (all), Sulawesi (all), Maluku (all), and Papua. PODES covers all provinces, whereas the IFLS only samples 13 provinces. So while this grouping is comprehensive only for PODES, when IFLS data are analyzed, each region includes only a few provinces. Hence, for IFLS: Sumatra—North Sumatra, West Sumatra, South Sumatra (including a newly established province that previously belonged to South Sumatra—Bangka Belitung), and Lampung; Java and Bali—all provinces including Banten; and Other Provinces—NTB, South Kalimantan, and South Sulawesi.

6. By definition a *desa siaga* is a village that has the resources capability and readiness to overcome health problems by mobilizing community resources. The *Desa Siaga* program was launched as a national program in 2006.

7. Information from the Human Resources Board for Health Professionals, DEPKES; administrative data source, personal communication 2008.

8. The IFLS is used as the database for this analysis because PODES does not have the information and IFLS allows trend analysis. The GDS provides similar results for 2006.

9. In addition to these permanently staffed facilities, an extensive outreach program of *posyandu* was established in nearly 250,000 villages between 1970 and 2005. *Posyandu* engage in monthly village gatherings at which community volunteers promote maternal and child health and nutrition and family planning activities.

10. These figures do not include hospitals belonging to the armed forces and the police or to other ministries or state-owned enterprises, which, although affiliated to state agencies, function more like private institutions.

11. Since decentralization in 2001, district hospitals are under the management of local government and are accountable to the *bupati* (elected official at the district level) and governor.

References

Barber, S. L., P. J. Gertler, and P. Harimurti. 2007a. "Differences in Access to High-Quality Outpatient Care in Indonesia." *Health Affairs* 26 (3): w352–66.

———. 2007b. "The Contribution of Human Resources for Health to the Quality of Care in Indonesia." *Health Affairs* 26 (3): w367–79.

Chomitz, K. M., G. Setiardi, A. Azwar, N. Ismail, and P. Widiyarti. 1998. "What Do Doctors Want? Developing Incentives for Doctors to Serve in Indonesia's Rural and Remote Areas." Policy Research Working Paper 1888, World Bank, Washington, DC.

Ensor, T., Z. Quayyum, M. Nadjib, and P. Sucahya. 2008. "Level and Determinants of Incentives for Village Midwives in Indonesia." *Health Policy and Planning* November 2008: 1–10.

IFLS (Indonesia Family Life Survey). 1997. http://www.rand.org/labor/FLS/IFLS.

———. 2007. http://www.rand.org/labor/FLS/IFLS.

MoH (Ministry of Health). 2007a. *Indonesian Health Profiles.* Jakarta: Ministry of Health. http://www.depkes.go.id/downloads/publikasi/Profil%20Kesehatan%20Indonesia%202007.pdf.

———. 2007b. *Indonesia's Hospital Statistics, Series I-IV.* Jakarta: Medical Service Information Unit.

PODES (Potensi Desa, [Survey of Village Potential]). 1996. Central Bureau of Statistics, Indonesia.

———. 2006. Central Bureau of Statistics, Indonesia.

Ruswendi, D. 2007. *Evaluation Study of the Deployment Policy for Contract (PTT) Doctors/Dentists in Remote Areas in 4 HWS Project Provinces: Kalimantan Barat; Kalimantan Timur; Sumatra Barat; Jambi. Year 2006–2007.* ADB Consultant Report. Manila: Asian Development Bank.

WHO (World Health Organization). 1978. *Alma Ata Conference Declaration.* http://who.int/hpr/NPH/docs/declaration_almaata.pdf.

World Bank. 2008. *Investing in Indonesia's Health: Challenges and Opportunities for Future Public Spending. Health Public Expenditure Review 2008.* Report 46815-ID. Jakarta: World Bank.

———. 2009. *Indonesia's Doctors, Midwives and Nurses: Current Stock, Increasing Needs, Future Challenges and Options.* Jakarta: World Bank.

CHAPTER 4

Effects of Changes in the Supply of Health Workers on the Use of Health Services

This chapter analyzes changes in the use of health services over time, overall, and by type of provider. What exactly drives increases in service utilization is a complicated question, but some econometric evidence from the Indonesia Family Life Survey (IFLS) panel data provides important insight. Generally it is expected that when the supply of and access to providers increase, use of health services will increase. Moreover, as wealth and disposable income rise, the demand for services is also likely to increase.[1] In this chapter, patterns in the overall use of outpatient and inpatient services are described, followed by a more thorough analysis of changes in the choice of provider.

Patterns in the Use of Services and Changes in Provider Choice, 1997–2007

Utilization rates for health care increased only slightly over the 1997–2007 period, but the modest increase probably masks more dramatic changes. In other words, using IFLS for 1997, and subsequently IFLS for 2007, provides only a snapshot of utilization at two points in time and does not capture dynamics in utilization rates over the decade. Adding the IFLS 2000 data (table 4.1) shows that a substantial drop in utilization occurred during and

Table 4.1   Changes in Utilization of Health Services versus Self-Medication
(*percent*)

Region	Outpatient utilization	Inpatient utilization	Self-medication: OTC medicine
All sample 1997	19.13	2.15	59.94
Sumatra	15.51	1.69	56.98
Java and Bali	20.35	2.44	60.80
Other Provinces	18.53	1.64	60.03
All sample 2000	14.60	2.31	31.85
Sumatra	14.73	2.45	31.24
Java and Bali	14.91	2.42	33.60
Other Provinces	13.57	1.84	27.32
All sample 2007	21.09	3.18	59.82
Sumatra	19.01	3.69	58.13
Java and Bali	22.45	3.09	58.86
Other Provinces	17.83	2.96	58.59

Source: IFLS 1997, 2007, http://www.rand.org/labor/FLS/IFLS.
Note: OTC = over-the-counter.

in the immediate aftermath of the 1997–98 financial and economic crisis, which postdated the 1997 IFLS survey, and that a considerable increase is apparent again by 2007. The drop in utilization following the crisis is important to keep in mind: utilization dropped by nearly 30 percent and remained low until July 2005, when *Askeskin*, the health insurance program for the poor now called *Jamkesmas*, was introduced.[2]

Using IFLS data, one observes increases in overall utilization of health service facilities and in self-treatment between 1997 and 2007. Of those who were ill, 19.1 percent sought inpatient care at a facility in 1997, while 21.1 percent did so in 2007 (table 4.1). The increase in utilization took place in Java and Bali and in Sumatra provinces, but actually dropped in Other Provinces. Inpatient services increased more significantly, from 2.2 percent in 1997 to 3.2 percent in 2007, and increases were recorded everywhere, including in Other Provinces.

Even as utilization increased, a large proportion of the population relies on self-treatment or forgoes any treatment at all, and the percentages remained the same over the period. Two-thirds of Indonesia's population still relies on self-treatment when ill. Although that may not necessarily be a negative finding, as it is not always necessary to visit a health provider for a common disease, the very high use of over-the-counter (OTC) drugs and the quality of those drugs are of concern. Indonesia experiences high rates of illegal sales of prescription drugs by unlicensed drugstores, informal outlets, physicians, and other health practitioners (Hawkins et al. 2009).

Except for Other Provinces, the patterns of increasing utilization are similar for all regions and by per capita expenditure (PCE) quintiles in both surveys. It is notable that the largest increase appears to have taken place in the poorer two quintiles (table 4.2). Between 1997 and 2007, outpatient utilization among the poorest increased by almost 25 percent, from 15.3 percent to 19.0 percent. Considering the drop immediately after the financial crisis in 1997, reflected in the IFLS 2000 data, the increase reflects a doubling in the utilization rate from the years just after the crisis. These increases may in part reflect the effective implementation of the *Askeskin/Jamkesmas* program after 2005.[3]

Further analyses show that individuals living in households belonging to the top two quintiles of the district per capita expenditure distribution

Table 4.2   Changes in Inpatient and Outpatient Utilization by PCE Quintile

Region	PCE Quintile				
	1st (poorest)	2nd	3rd	4th	5th (richest)
Outpatient					
Full sample 1997	15.34	18.01	19.83	20.33	23.32
Full sample 2000	11.54	12.63	16.46	15.34	18.36
Full sample 2007	18.92	19.93	20.59	21.99	24.30
Sumatra 1997	11.73	11.43	17.12	17.36	21.31
Sumatra 2000	11.38	13.74	15.34	15.49	18.72
Sumatra 2007	17.49	18.03	18.39	18.40	22.07
Java and Bali 1997	16.81	20.18	20.96	21.09	24.06
Java and Bali 2000	11.76	12.90	17.19	15.91	18.29
Java and Bali 2007	19.90	21.64	21.91	23.31	26.09
Other Provinces 1997	13.64	17.48	18.50	20.86	22.77
Other Provinces 2000	11.06	10.77	15.44	13.53	18.20
Other Provinces 2007	16.32	14.62	17.45	20.76	19.44
Inpatient					
Full sample 1997	1.48	1.55	1.61	2.05	3.06
Full sample 2000	1.57	1.88	2.27	2.79	3.35
Full sample 2007	2.03	2.58	2.56	3.24	3.88
Sumatra 1997	1.15	1.38	1.31	0.87	1.90
Sumatra 2000	1.28	2.23	2.37	3.11	3.42
Sumatra 2007	2.12	2.78	2.34	3.67	4.87
Java and Bali 1997	1.17	1.81	1.79	2.68	3.61
Java and Bali 2000	1.68	1.99	2.36	2.71	3.82
Java and Bali 2007	2.18	2.65	2.83	3.08	4.00
Other Provinces 1997	1.18	0.68	1.28	1.10	2.43
Other Provinces 2000	1.50	1.20	1.91	2.69	2.04
Other Provinces 2007	1.37	2.12	1.84	3.42	2.38

Source: IFLS 1997, 2007, http://www.rand.org/labor/FLS/IFLS.

were more likely to use a health care provider when ill in 2007.[4] For the lowest three quintiles, there is no statistically significant effect of socioeconomic status on utilization. It is important to remember that these models show the effects of position in the within-district distribution of consumption, after controlling for years of schooling. Education is positively associated with health care utilization for two reasons: first, more-educated individuals tend to have higher levels of permanent income and may be able to borrow or draw down savings to cover the cost, and second, it is likely that education is systematically related to knowledge about the importance of health care.

Utilization patterns of poorer and richer residents of the community also changed between 1997 and 2007.[5] The analysis suggests a 3.6 percent increase in the probability that the poorest 20 percent of residents in a community use a health services provider when ill. A smaller increase in utilization of 2.1 percent occurred for households in the 2nd to 4th quintiles of the consumption distribution. The highest PCE quintiles also saw an increase in the likelihood of seeking care.

Choice of Providers

In 1997, the *puskesmas* was the provider of choice for close to 40 percent of those reporting having been ill.[6] About 23 percent preferred a private physician, and another 23 percent a private midwife or nurse (table 4.3). By 2007, a shift occurred toward use of midwives, with the largest share seeking care from private midwives and nurses (30 percent), then the *puskesmas* (29 percent), and only 20 percent using private physicians. Table 4.4 illustrates the findings on changes in type of provider used, by per capita expenditure quintiles.[7] The decline in utilization is almost universal in all the income groups, but not for all providers, except for the poorest quintiles who, despite a serious decline, continued to use *puskesmas* as the preferred provider in almost 40 percent of cases. The richer quintiles used *puskesmas* much less.

In 1997, 45 percent of the relatively poor (1st PCE quintile) and a similar percentage of the near-poor (2nd PCE quintile) who were ill sought treatment at a *puskesmas*. By 2007, the percentages had fallen to less than 40 percent of the poorest and 33 percent of the near-poor. They did not go to the private practitioners, whose utilization also declined, but a large increase in use of private midwives and nurses and traditional practitioners occurred. In 1997, some 24 percent of the poor and 21 percent of the near-poor visited private midwives or nurses; the figures rose to 31 percent

Table 4.3   Choice of Provider of Outpatient Services when Ill
(percent)

Region	Public hospital	Puskesmas and pustu	Private hospital	Private clinic	Private physician	Nurse, midwife	Traditional practitioner
Full sample							
1997	4.65	39.15	3.25	4.15	23.31	22.91	2.07
Sumatra	4.97	40.06	5.57	4.07	18.52	23.64	2.86
Java and Bali	4.44	35.23	3.44	4.55	27.34	23.35	1.14
Other Provinces	5.28	55.90	0.00	2.48	10.09	20.19	5.43
Full sample							
2007	4.06	29.40	3.13	5.26	19.46	30.10	8.36
Sumatra	4.40	23.32	3.37	4.92	16.58	37.44	9.49
Java and Bali	3.76	29.16	3.34	6.07	20.95	28.78	7.64
Other Provinces	5.32	38.54	1.00	1.33	15.12	27.74	10.80

Source: IFLS 1997, 2007, http://www.rand.org/labor/FLS/IFLS.

Table 4.4   Outpatient Services Utilization by Type and PCE Quintile

Quintile	Public hospital	Puskesmas and pustu	Private hospital	Private clinic	Private physician	Nurse, midwife	Traditional practitioner
Full sample							
1997	4.65	39.15	3.25	4.15	23.31	22.91	2.07
Poorest, 1st quintile	3.69	45.35	2.80	4.46	18.09	23.69	1.91
2nd quintile	2.84	43.61	3.48	4.52	21.16	21.03	3.35
3rd quintile	4.47	41.01	2.00	3.17	23.50	24.44	1.41
4th quintile	5.40	37.11	3.30	5.07	24.12	23.02	1.98
Richest, 5th quintile	6.68	31.18	4.69	3.75	28.60	23.21	1.88
Full sample							
2007	4.06	29.40	3.13	5.26	19.46	30.10	8.36
Poorest, 1st quintile	2.74	39.84	1.60	3.54	14.73	30.48	7.08
2nd quintile	3.37	32.33	1.80	4.45	17.31	32.81	7.93
3rd quintile	4.67	30.72	3.15	6.54	17.52	28.62	8.76
4th quintile	3.83	24.97	3.72	5.84	20.40	33.05	8.18
Richest, 5th quintile	5.52	21.77	4.48	5.94	26.98	26.56	8.75

Source: IFLS 1997, 2007, http://www.rand.org/labor/FLS/IFLS.

of the poor and 33 percent of the near-poor in 2007. Among the richer quintiles, most also sought treatment from a midwife or nurse when ill, rather than from private practitioners. In addition, utilization of traditional practitioners increased among all income quintiles (table 4.4).

The overall increase in use of private services is surprising, as is the corresponding decline in use of public services, since a number of changes and new policies would have been expected to increase the use of public facilities. A few hypotheses may explain these findings.

1. The *Askeskin/Jamkesmas* program would have been expected to increase utilization of public health services because its beneficiaries are encouraged to use public facilities.[8] *Askeskin/Jamkesmas* provides extra resources to the *puskesmas* on a capitation basis that considers the number of poor people in the catchment area. The funds are intended to cover the costs of the poor, who are entitled to free health care at the primary as well as the secondary level. The extra resources are not, however, linked to patients or to performance or payment systems that would encourage health staff at the *puskesmas* to provide more and better services or specifically to encourage the poor to seek treatment. Capitation payments are based on the number of poor on a prospective basis, not on actual utilization by patients with *Askeskin/Jamkesmas* cards.

2. Although the *Askeskin/Jamkesmas* program aims to increase use of services by the poor through the removal of financial barriers, other barriers remain.[9] The poor continue to incur substantial indirect and nonfinancial cost barriers, such as transportation costs and travel time to the *puskesmas*. The decline in public services and increased use of private services may occur in part because private midwives and nurses are geographically closer to the beneficiaries than are the *puskesmas*.

3. The utilization effects of *Askeskin/Jamkesmas* may be underestimated. Program coverage and knowledge about the program remained limited in the first few years, and the IFLS fieldwork was conducted during the second year of the program. Alternatively, patients may have bypassed the *puskesmas* and gone directly to public or private hospitals directly with the *Askeskin/Jamkesmas* card, a phenomenon that has been described anecdotally but that cannot be verified from available observational data.

4. Another hypothesis is that reduced use of *puskesmas* is due to the lack of health workers. Since 1997, the number of *puskesmas* without

doctors has increased, and the numbers of midwives and nurses per *puskesmas* also declined from 1997 to 2007. Besides the lack of staff, overall quality of care is also a concern that may lead to less utilization.

5. Although the supply of *puskesmas* steadily increased over the study period (MoH 2007a), likely improving access, that better access did not lead to higher utilization might be explained by the fact that the population ratio planning method that the Ministry of Health uses does not adequately capture demand for care.

Recent studies by Sparrow, Suryahadi, and Widjanti (2008) and Kruse, Pradhan, and Sparrow (2009) show a positive effect of *Askeskin/Jamkesmas* on the utilization of public services, particularly among the poor, who are the beneficiaries of the Health Insurance for the Poor program. That IFLS does not include the poorest provinces may explain the differences between IFLS and *Susenas* results. There is support for this explanation when the analysis is conducted using *Susenas* data, but with only the provinces that were also included in IFLS. Soon after the 1997–98 financial and economic crisis, the utilization of health services overall declined significantly, by about one-third. According to *Susenas* 2000, utilization of *puskesmas* and *pustu* declined by about two-thirds from 1997 (table 4.5).

Increases in the use of public facilities between 1997 and 2007 were especially large in non–IFLS provinces, but the increase between 2002 and 2007 was smaller than the national average. This may explain why the national averages suggest different patterns than the IFLS. Poorer, eastern Indonesian provinces are likely to see a larger effect of the Health Insurance for the Poor program, since a large part of the population received *Askeskin/Jamkesmas* cards and uses them at the public facilities.

Another surprising finding was that despite increases in the supply of physicians, the use of private physicians declined between 1997 and 2007 (table 4.4). Even though use of private clinics increased, that does not make up for the decline.[10] The only exception to this phenomenon occurred in Other Provinces, where the use of private physicians increased by one-third. The largest decline in use of private physicians occurred in Java and Bali, while in Other Provinces their use increased from 10 percent to 15 percent. The supply of private physicians in Other Provinces did increase, although not at a significantly higher rate than in Java and Bali or in Sumatra. *Susenas* data for the IFLS provinces show the same trend but with smaller declines and increases.

Table 4.5 Choice of Outpatient Services Provider when Ill

(percentage of those seeking treatment)

Sample	Public hospital	Puskesmas and pustu	Private hospital	Private clinic	Private physician	Paramedics (incl. nurse and midwife)	Traditional practitioner
All IFLS provinces 1997	2.12	22.53	1.64	1.55	13.85	12.41	2.45
Non–IFLS 1997	3.91	33.10	1.76	1.92	8.21	10.02	2.89
All IFLS provinces 2000	1.99	12.59	1.49	1.28	11.32	9.32	1.15
Non–IFLS 2000	1.96	17.10	1.68	1.24	6.80	6.47	1.12
All IFLS provinces 2007	2.44	14.96	1.76	—	13.76	13.92	0.82
Non–IFLS 2007	3.13	21.26	1.37	—	8.40	8.09	0.58

Source: *Susenas* (national household survey conducted by Indonesia's Central Bureau of Statistics, BPS) 1997, 2000, 2007; http://www.rand.org/labor/bps/susenas/.
Note: — = not available.

In contrast, a significant increase occurred in use of private midwives and nurses. Whereas the use of *puskesmas* and private physicians decreased, it appears that patients were more likely to seek treatment from midwives and nurses. Simultaneously, the number of midwives, and probably also of nurses, grew significantly. Midwives and nurses are also more evenly distributed, often residing close to their patients in the areas where they practice. With increased supply at closer proximity to the patient, it is likely that people who are ill seek treatment nearby, rather than traveling to the *puskesmas* or to private physicians who may be both more expensive and farther away.

Interestingly, the traditional practitioner is the preferred provider for almost 10 percent of those who are ill, even among the richer quintiles. Among those seeking treatment, the number choosing traditional practitioners increased fourfold, to more than 8 percent (table 4.3).[11] It is known that traditional healers are very popular in Indonesia. More microstudies of their use and quality would be beneficial. One hypothesis to consider in this regard is the link with the increasing incidence of noncommunicable disease, for which even the richer quintiles may resort to alternative care when modern medicine does not yield obvious improvements in health.

Changes in the Supply of Private Health Services and Utilization

The growth of the private sector has contributed to an increase in the supply of health service providers. The increase may reduce congestion and wait times at clinics, whether public or private. Reducing this cost may encourage increased use of services. Households less able to cover the fees of private physicians may not use health facilities or may seek care from poorer-quality providers. As shown in table 4.4 above, poorer members of IFLS communities are more likely to use public providers. Table 4.6 presents the results of multivariate analyses showing the effects of increases in private physician practices on the utilization of services and on choice of provider.

Expansion of the private sector is associated with increased use of all outpatient services among the poorest two quintiles by 3.1 percent and 3.5 percent, respectively.[12] The association between the private sector and utilization of outpatient services is stronger in rural areas than in urban areas for both men and women. When one examines the data on private physicians and midwives separately, the number of private doctors per 100,000 residents is more strongly associated with increased utilization

Table 4.6   Effect of Increasing the Number of Private Physicians on Probability that the Poor Will Visit a Facility when Ill

Sample	Effect on probability of using health services	Effect on probability of using public outpatient services
All observations	0.041**	0.165***
	(0.017)	(0.044)
Urban		
Male	0.046*	0.150*
	(0.028)	(0.086)
Female	0.023	0.012
	(0.029)	(0.069)
Rural		
Male	0.172***	0.501***
	(0.057)	(0.146)
Female	0.113**	0.069
	(0.057)	(0.146)

Source: Authors.
Note: This table shows the increased probability that the poor will use health services and public outpatient services when the number of private physician practices in the community increases by 1 per 100,000. Here the poor are the lowest 20 percent of the PCE distribution within the community. Specifically, the table presents coefficients for the lowest quintile. The table shows coefficients from the doctor interaction term shown in Model 2 of appendix tables A4.1 through A4.10. Standard errors of the estimated effect are shown in parentheses. *** indicates significance at the 1 percent level, ** at 5 percent, and * at 10 percent. For more information on the models estimated, including other characteristics included as controls, see the discussion in appendix 4.

among the poor.[13] As shown in table 4.6, an increase in the number of private physician practices per 100,000 residents is associated with an even more pronounced increase in health service utilization by the poorer members of the community.

Although a greater number of private providers is associated with expanded utilization of health services by the relatively poor, the poor are more likely to choose the public *puskesmas* when an increase in private physician practice occurs.[14] This finding suggests that a process of sorting affluent patients to private providers takes place with an increase in private practice. Sorting is likely to occur both through the market and through encouragement by *puskesmas* physicians with private practices on the side. More affluent members of the community may self-select to a private provider whose office setting is more appealing and has shorter wait times or more convenient hours of operation. A *puskesmas* physician may also directly encourage affluent patients to come to their private practice and pay a higher fee while providing care to poorer members of the community at the *puskesmas*. When the sample is split into rural and urban areas, further evidence of sorting of patients appears. More specifi-cally, after controlling for the effects of other characteristics affecting uti-lization (such as age, education, family demographics, gender, and geographic location), adding one private physician practice per 100,000 people is associated with a 16.5 percent increase in the probability that residents in the poorest PCE quintile will use a public facility (table 4.6) and an 8.5 percent reduction in the probability that those in the richest quintile will do so (appendix table A4.6).

Although a positive association is observed between an increase in the number of private sector midwives and utilization, it is not statistically significant for the poorest 20 percent of the community. The reason that the correlation is not strong may be that programs to expand the number of midwives may be less systematically related to observed demand for health services. The main nationwide public programs, such as the BDD, were not purely demand based. In contrast, the increase in the number of private physicians, particularly those providing mostly or entirely pri-vate services, is likely to be more demand driven. Although midwives are increasingly becoming private and making choices based on private opportunities, the link between more private midwives and higher levels of utilization may not be picked up here because the phenomenon is more recent.

Notes

1. Indonesia's GDP has grown since the 1997–98 financial and economic crisis at an average rate of 5 percent, bringing reductions in poverty and improved household income.

2. *Askeskin/Jamkesmas* insurance contributed to an increase in utilization of health services both in general and among the poor (World Bank 2008). Differences between IFLS findings and *Susenas* (the national household survey conducted by Indonesia's Central Bureau of Statistics, BPS, at http://www .rand.org/labor/bps/susenas/) for the same years can be explained by coverage: IFLS does not cover eastern Indonesia, except for a few provinces, whereas *Susenas* is a national survey. To analyze utilization by the same households and individuals over time, IFLS data were used in this study.

3. Although IFLS allows for analysis in much greater depth of the impact of *Askeskin/Jamkesmas* and utilization, such an analysis goes beyond the scope of this report and will be described in subsequent publications under the broader Health Sector Reform Agenda development.

4. These are the results from the base model provided in appendix 4, table A4.1, Model 1.

5. These results were derived from appendix 4, table A4.1, Model 2.

6. For those reporting being ill and using outpatient services, the IFLS question refers to services used over the past 4 weeks, whereas inpatient utilization figures are calculated based on estimates of use over the past 12 months.

7. Within-district per capita expenditure quintiles were calculated from the distribution of non-health care expenditures within the district.

8. A 2008 paper by Sparrow, Suryahadi, and Widjanti indeed shows a positive effect from the *Askeskin/Jamkesmas* program on utilization of public services. Their analysis, however, uses *Susenas*, which is representative nationally, whereas the IFLS does not cover eastern Indonesia.

9. The work by Sparrow, Suryahadi, and Widjanti (2008) shows an increase in utilization of public services among the poor. This can be explained by their use of *Susenas* data, which include the poorer provinces, where utilization of public services by the poor may be higher.

10. For detailed descriptions of what constitutes a public and a private clinic, see appendix 2 on definitions of health facilities.

11. In this finding there is a discrepancy between *Susenas* and IFLS findings, as shown in appendix 4 tables A4.12 and A4.13, that may be explained by difference in definitions of traditional healers.

12. Model 1 of table A4.1 in appendix 4 shows the results from estimating the effects of the private sector on outpatient utilization of health care by all types of providers.

13. See appendix 4, tables A4.2 to A4.5.

14. The relatively affluent are more likely to seek care from the private sector. See appendix 4, table A4.6.

References

Hawkins, L., P. Harimurti, C. Rokx, and P. Marzoeki. 2009. *Policy Note on Pharmaceutical Sector in Indonesia*. Policy Note Series. Jakarta: World Bank.

IFLS (Indonesia Family Life Survey). 1997. http://www.rand.org/labor/FLS/IFLS.

———. 2007. http://www.rand.org/labor/FLS/IFLS.

Kruse, I., M. Pradhan, and R. Sparrow. 2009. "Marginal Benefit Incidence of Public Health Spending: Evidence from Indonesian Sub-national Data." Working Paper 487, Institute of Social Studies, The Netherlands.

MoH (Ministry of Health). 2007a. *Indonesian Health Profiles*. Jakarta: Ministry of Health. http://www.depkes.go.id/downloads/publikasi/Profil%20Kesehatan%20Indonesia%202007.pdf.

———. 2007b. *Indonesia's Hospital Statistics, Series I-IV.* Jakarta: Medical Service Information Unit.

Sparrow, R., A. Suryahadi, and W. Widjanti. 2008. *Public Health Insurance for the Poor: Targeting and Impact of Indonesia's ASKESKIN Program.* Paper presented at the ABCDE 2008 conference in Cape Town, South Africa.

Susenas (national household survey conducted by Indonesia's Central Bureau of Statistics, BPS). 1997. http://www.rand.org/labor/bps/susenas/.

———. 2000. http://www.rand.org/labor/bps/susenas/).

———. 2007. http://www.rand.org/labor/bps/susenas/).

World Bank. 2008. *Investing in Indonesia's Health: Challenges and Opportunities for Future Public Spending. Health Public Expenditure Review 2008.* Jakarta: World Bank.

CHAPTER 5

The Quality of Public Health Facilities and Practitioners

Although the *supply* of health services has significantly improved, the Indonesian government has only very recently started to concentrate on improving the *quality* of health services. Of most importance have been (a) changes in medical education policies, by which the government is trying to increase its oversight, and (b) further clarification of the role of local governments in the recruitment and deployment of medical staff and the implications of their responsibilities for the quality of care.

At present, however, serious quality concerns remain about the education system itself and the subsequent certification and accreditation of health workers; a serious shortfall in capacity also exists. Although some systems have been established, such as systems to accredit medical, midwifery, and nursing schools, accreditation is not done by an independent body, and professionals capable of performing accreditations are in short supply. The standards themselves are also deficient, making accreditation very difficult, and accreditations that have been conducted are not published. Guidelines for responsibilities within the regulatory system were not well delineated when government authority was decentralized in 2001. This situation has since worsened because some local governments now issue permits or licenses to schools to operate without obtaining a license from the Higher Education Directorate of the Ministry of National Education (MoNE).

This chapter discusses changes in the structural quality of health facilities and the diagnostic and treatment ability of all health providers, including *puskesmas* and *pustu* and the three types of private practitioners, as discussed in chapter 4. Diagnostic and treatment ability, an important dimension of quality, is measured from response scores on vignettes regarding prenatal, child curative, and adult curative care.[1]

In this chapter, policies affecting quality will be discussed where links with study findings appear evident; however, policy changes in the area of education have very-long-term effects. These policies mostly relate to health workforce education and in-service training, the accreditation of public as well as private educational institutions, and licensing of service providers. Provider payment systems, which can have shorter-term effects, are discussed when they are likely to have had an effect on the quality of the care provided, as are changes due to the decentralization of service delivery in 2001. Because a statistical analysis of these policies is not possible with the data available, their causal impact remains ambiguous. Exploring potential explanations for changes in quality is an important area for future policy research (box 5.1).

Changes in the Structural Quality of Public Health Facilities: *Puskesmas* and *Pustu*

Increased public funding from sources such as *Askeskin/Jamkesmas* (Health Insurance for the Poor) capitation funds has been made available at the *puskesmas* level, leading to improvements in environmental, hygiene, and sanitation standards. For example, all facilities had better access to water in 2007 (tables 5.1 and 5.2). Campaigns by international donor agencies such as the Global Fund and the World Health Organization, and the increased attention to specific immunization campaigns are also likely contributors. However, increased supply does not always translate directly into improved child immunization status. The most recent Demographic and Health Survey (BPS 2008) shows that measles immunization among children ages 12 to 23 months increased from 60 percent in 1997, to 67 percent in 2007, an improvement of only seven percentage points. The target rate of immunization is 90 percent.

The availability of vaccines at *pustu* improved during the 10 years from 1997 to 2007. In 1997, only 29 percent of *pustu* had measles vaccines and 33 percent had tetanus vaccines in stock. In 2007, the

Box 5.1

Food for Thought—Unpacking the Health Production Function: Quality and Health Outcomes

Improving the supply of health care and the quality of care providers are useful intermediate goals for strengthening the health system, and human resources in particular. Yet an evaluation of the effectiveness of policies to expand the supply and improve the quality of care providers should include assessments of whether the policies have any impact on health outcomes. Given recent increases in spending, and considering Indonesia's still-moderate performance on certain health indicators, research into the relationship between resources and outcomes is warranted. The IFLS data source is useful in this regard because it includes objective measures of health status. Here the focus is not on the supply of human resources, but on proxy measures of its quality.

Hemoglobin and Prenatal Care (Females, age 15–49)

	Level	*Level*
Year dummy (2007 = 1)	0.159***	0.159***
Prenatal vignette score (z-score)	0.044**	0.038*
Poorest 20%	−0.068	−0.067
Prenatal vignette score × Poorest 20%		0.034
Education (years)	−0.003	−0.003
Age (years)	−0.002	−0.002
Urban = 1	−0.036	−0.037
Constant	12.541***	12.541***
Observations	10,904	10,904
R-squared	0.056	0.057

Source: IFLS 1997, 2007, http://www.rand.org/labor/FLS/IFLS.
Note: Robust standard errors in brackets. ***$p < 0.01$, **$p < 0.05$, *$p < 0.10$. All models control for district fixed effects.

   Preliminary research focused on hemoglobin levels and iron deficiency anemia. Iron deficiency, as indicated by low hemoglobin (Hb), is associated with elevated susceptibility to disease and fatigue. Low hemoglobin may indicate that an individual suffers from treatable disorders, such as intestinal worms, and thus interaction with health care professionals could be expected to reduce the incidence of low hemoglobin. A substantial literature demonstrates that iron deficiency anemia results in reduced work capacity and may thus affect economic well-being (Thomas et al. 2007). It is likely that this measure,

(continued)

Box 5.1 *(continued)*

like many other health outcomes, is affected by access to care, competence of health care providers, and medical treatment. Data from the 1997 wave of IFLS indicate the potential significance of anemia in Indonesia. A third of reproductive-age women (age 15 to 49) were found to have low levels of iron, as indicated by Hb levels below 120g/L, or grams per liter, the cutoff recommended by the World Health Organization.

To examine whether changes in the diagnostic and treatment abilities of health providers translate into improved health outcomes, the relationship between provider scores on diagnostic and treatment vignettes and hemoglobin levels of women of child-bearing age were examined. Women are the focus here because their use of health care increased between 1997 and 2007, and objective health measures from the IFLS, such as hemoglobin, map into improvements in diagnostic and treatment ability that would be captured by prenatal care and adult curative care vignettes.

Results are shown in the accompanying table. They reveal a positive association between z-score on the prenatal vignette and hemoglobin levels. A one standard deviation increase in score on the prenatal vignette is associated with an increase from 0.038 to 0.044 in hemoglobin levels. In terms of reducing anemia, then, we find that a one standard deviation increase in the health care provider prenatal vignette score is associated with a 2 percent decline in the probability that a woman in the lowest per capital expenditure quintile will be suffering from anemia.

percentages almost doubled, and more than half of *pustu* now have measles and tetanus vaccines. However, tuberculosis treatment has worsened since 1997. In 1997, 53 percent of *pustu* provided tuberculosis (TB) treatment, but only 30 percent did so in 2007. It is unclear why this situation has worsened. Possible explanations include fewer staff at *pustus* than in 1997, reduced availability of drugs, lack of operating funds after decentralization—even though capitation funds from *Askeskin/Jamkesmas* could be used for health promotion—and government prioritization of maternal health as a main intervention, which may have diverted attention from other public health programs, such as the one to counter TB.

Physicians working in private practices performed worse on both vaccine availability and TB treatment in 2007 than in 1997. This is difficult

Table 5.1   Structural Indicators and Quality Scores for Prenatal, Child Curative, and Adult Curative Care in 2007, by Clinical Setting
(percent)

Quality measures	Public settings		Private settings			
	Puskesmas	Pustu	Private nurse	Private midwife	Private physician	All settings
Structural quality						
Internal water source	89	71	80	84	89	84
Inpatient beds	28	3	3	28	3	18
Functioning microscope	79	5	1	3	7	25
Tuberculosis service[a]	95	30	8	2	44	38
Measles vaccines in stock	97	51	5	48	11	51
Tetanus toxoid vaccine in stock	97	55	9	59	12	55
Hepatitis B vaccine in stock	92	52	6	54	16	52

Source: IFLS 2007, http://www.rand.org/labor/FLS/IFLS.
a. The question asked was whether medical treatment for tuberculosis is available.

Table 5.2   Structural Indicators and Quality Scores for Prenatal, Child Curative, and Adult Curative Care in 1997, by Clinical Setting
(percent)

Quality measures	Public settings		Private settings			
	Puskesmas	Pustu	Private nurse	Private midwife	Private physician	All settings
Structural quality						
Internal water source	65	33	67	76	76	66
Inpatient beds	18	0	1	19	2	10
Functioning microscope	81	0	1	2	8	22
Tuberculosis service	96	53	16	6	56	46
Measles vaccines in stock	94	29	4	43	21	41
Tetanus toxoid vaccine in stock	94	33	6	60	23	46
Hepatitis B vaccine in stock	92	25	4	36	25	39

Source: Barber, Gertler, and Harimurti 2007a, using IFLS 1997.

to explain, as current policy is focused specifically on greater involvement by the private sector in TB control. These findings merit more analysis, follow-up to gain a better understanding of explanations, and subsequent recommendations for policy changes.

Measuring Diagnostic Ability Using Indonesia Family Life Survey Vignettes

The ability of health providers to diagnose illness correctly is measured using community and facility health vignette questions from the Indonesia Family Life Survey (IFLS, http://www.rand.org/labor/FLS/IFLS/) 1997 and 2007. The interviewer presents the health vignette or case to the health worker and asks how the worker would proceed. At the *puskesmas*, the highest-ranking health worker available at the time of the visit is interviewed, and in private settings the physician, midwife, or nurse is interviewed.

Three vignettes are related to diagnosis and treatment of conditions common in prenatal, child, and adult care, respectively. For example, one vignette has a mother bringing in a child suffering from diarrhea for more than two days. Among the items that the interviewer records is an indication of whether the health provider takes the temperature of the patient, asks about frequency of diarrhea, and asks about the nature of the stool. (Presence of blood in the stool, for example, helps to distinguish viral diarrhea from dysentery.)[2] The interviewer then assigns a score of one for a correct answer or zero for an incorrect or missing answer to a prepared list of items based on standards for diagnosis and treatment. Two types of quality scores are constructed for each health case: the raw score, which is the share of correct responses multiplied by 100, and the normalized raw score, or z-score, which shows the difference from the mean in the category divided by the standard deviation.[3]

Using 1997 IFLS data, Barber, Gertler, and Harimurti (2007a) found that *puskesmas*-based health providers had above average diagnostic ability in prenatal care. They also found that physicians in private practice were of higher ability in diagnosing child and adult illnesses. Nurses providing private services had below average ability on all vignettes, as did most providers, public and private, in the more remote and poor areas in 1997. The 2007 IFLS also included the health worker vignettes and thus allows analysis of changes over time in the diagnostic ability of service providers. Moreover, by linking community-level information on diagnostic and treatment ability, it is possible to examine the relationships between quality, utilization, and health outcomes and changes in policies affecting human resources for health care.

It should be noted that for the public sector, only *puskesmas* and *pustu* are included, whereas private practitioner ratings were obtained for nurses, midwives, and physicians. At public health facilities, the vignettes were conducted with the highest-level health worker present when enumerators arrived to conduct the facility survey, and their responses are used as the *puskesmas* or *pustu* score. In cases where no physician was present, the person questioned could have been a midwife, paramedic, or nurse, which is considered representative of the quality of care provided at that facility at that time.[4] Interviewers were careful to visit public facilities during public working hours. Finally, the vignettes reflect the diagnostic and treatment abilities of basic health care providers and do not include more sophisticated care at secondary and tertiary levels. Hospital care is not discussed in this study.

Changes in Diagnostic and Treatment Ability over Time

Between 1997 and 2007, statistically significant, but small, improvements occurred in scores on diagnostic and treatment ability in both urban and rural areas of all regions, for all three health conditions, and in both the public and the private sector (see table 5.3 for standard requirements). The scores shown in table 5.4 represent the percentage scored correctly on the vignette. For example, when the case is a sick child with fever, if the health worker correctly mentions all standard diagnostic and treatment practices that should be employed in such a case, the score would be 100 percent.

The scores on the prenatal care vignettes in both the public and the private health sector improved by four percentage points between 1997 and 2007, with the greatest improvement taking place in Other Provinces. Quality of child curative care shows similar improvements, both in magnitude and across regions, but started from a higher base in 1997. In 2007, the highest child curative care scores were found in public facilities in Java and Bali, with an average score of 66 percent on diagnostic and treatment ability standards.

Diagnostic and treatment abilities in public facilities improved most for child care, whereas private practitioners had more pronounced improvements for adult care. The highest diagnostic ability for adult curative care was found in Java and Bali; the lowest was found in Sumatra, despite Sumatra's recording the most significant improvement over the period. Sumatra is consistently below the national average score and shows the lowest-quality diagnostic and treatment ability for all three conditions.

Among the different facilities and practitioners, the best score for prenatal diagnostic ability and treatment standards was found at the

Table 5.3   Clinical Case Required Standards of Diagnostic and Treatment Practice

Prenatal care	Care for an adult with respiratory infection	Care of a child with diarrhea and vomiting
Evaluate hypertensive disorders	*Take history*	*Take history*
Ask history of high blood pressure	Ask about duration of illness	Ask about duration of illness
Take blood pressure	Ask about previous respiratory illnesses	Ask about frequency of illness
Test urine protein	Ask about blood in cough	Ask about appearance of stools/vomit
Ask about smoking habit	Ask about color of sputum	Ask about blood in stools
Take history and physical	Ask about chest pain	Ask about fever
Ask about history of heart disease	*Conduct physical sputum*	*Conduct physical*
Ask about history of diabetes	Take temperature	Take temperature
Ask about family history of illnesses	Listen to respiration	Check for sunken fontanelles
Take height measurements	Examine ears	Check skin turgor
Weigh patient	Assess chest indrawing	Take pulse
Measure uterine height	Assess for cyanosis	Check alertness
Assess whether high-risk pregnancy	Test sputum	*Provide care and advice*
Perform diagnostics and prevention		Administer oral rehydration fluids
Determine tetanus immunization status		Recommend when to return if worse
Test for sexually transmitted infections		
Test hemoglobin levels		
Advise on nutrition		
Give iron-folate		
Establish case management system		
Date the pregnancy		
Plan for delivery		
Plan for follow-up visits		

Source: IFLS 1997, 2007. http://www.rand.org/labor/FLS/IFLS.

puskesmas, but little difference between the *puskesmas* and private midwives and physicians is apparent (table 5.5).[5] The highest scores on child care vignettes were found among private physicians and respondents at the *puskesmas*. The scores on the diagnostic and treatment standards are also shown separately for urban and rural areas in table 5.5 but reveal few differences between the areas. This is not entirely unexpected, as providers in both areas are the products of similar preservice education institutions.

Table 5.4   Quality of Public Health Services in Indonesia, 1997–2007, by Region

	National setting			Java and Bali			Sumatra			Other Provinces		
Service	1997	2007	P=	1997	2007	P=	1997	2007	P=	1997	2007	P=
Prenatal care												
Public	42	46	***	45	47	**	35	39	**	38	49	***
Private	40	44	***	43	46	***	34	37	**	39	46	***
Child curative care												
Public	56	64	***	58	66	***	48	56	***	55	65	***
Private	55	59	***	57	62	***	50	52		54	60	***
Adult curative care												
Public	49	56	***	52	59	***	43	48	***	44	53	***
Private	46	53	***	48	56	***	40	51	***	44	51	***

Source: IFLS 1997, 2007, http://www.rand.org/labor/FLS/IFLS. All models control for district fixed effects.
*** $p < 0.01$, ** $p < 0.05$, * $p < 0.10$.

Table 5.5   Detailed Quality Scores for Prenatal, Child Curative, and Adult Curative Care by Urban–Rural and Public–Private Setting

	Public settings		Private settings			
Quality measures	Puskesmas	Pustu	Private nurse	Private midwife	Private physician	All settings
Prenatal care	46	44	34	45	45	45
Urban	46	42	36	45	45	46
Rural	47	45	34	44	44	44
Child curative care	66	59	57	61	67	63
Urban	66	59	56	62	67	63
Rural	66	59	58	62	66	62
Adult care	58	49	47	48	59	54
Urban	58	51	47	47	59	55
Rural	58	51	49	49	59	52

Source: IFLS 2007, http://www.rand.org/labor/FLS/IFLS.

The improvements in health providers' diagnostic ability may be related to better access to in-service training, information, and educational and financial resources. More training institutions are operating, and access to information is better than it was a decade ago. Overall, 2007 scores on diagnostic and treatment vignettes were higher in public facilities than in private ones, but the private sector is catching up. The public sector has better in-service training opportunities, and that may be the reason that public sector facilities score higher.

The share of providers with dual practices is very high, and the provision of both public and private services by the same practitioner may explain some convergence in diagnostic ability. The changes in diagnostic ability over time are small but significant and merit analysis in greater depth. Although such an analysis would go beyond the scope of this study, a first cut is presented in appendix 2. Some more concrete illustrations of quality of diagnostic and treatment ability are shown in table 5.6, which lists the percentages of the detailed quality scores for all three vignettes by health provider, *puskesmas, pustu,* and private practitioners.

When one analyzes the more detailed standards of the prenatal care vignettes, stark differences appear between the abilities of *puskesmas* health workers and midwives, on the one hand, and private physicians on the other. Where only 28 percent of private physicians responded that they would measure blood pressure during a prenatal care visit, 89 percent of *puskesmas* health workers and private midwives would do so. Only 18 percent of private physicians responded that they would measure uterine height, as opposed to 66 percent of *puskesmas* health workers and private midwives.

Prenatal care provided by private nurses shows very low quality scores. Pregnant women in Indonesia have high levels of anemia, and provision of iron-folate is part of the required minimum service standards for all pregnant women, regardless of their anemia status. Although 72 percent of *puskesmas* health workers and 55 percent of midwives reported assessing hemoglobin level, only 42 percent of *puskesmas* health workers and 35 percent of midwives provide iron-folate.

Private physicians compare more favorably to *puskesmas* health workers on a number of diagnostic and treatment practices in child curative care, although at the same time overall scores are on the low side. Aggregate vignette scores show small differences among the providers, but when the more detailed standards are analyzed clear differences emerge. For example, as part of the child curative care vignette, an indicative question is whether the care provider asks about the nature of the stool when a child has diarrhea. Only 42 percent of *puskesmas* health workers and 43 percent of private physicians responded that they would ask this question. Even fewer private nurses and midwives reported that they would do so. Oral rehydration fluids are administered by 79 percent of *puskesmas* and *pustu* health workers and by 74 percent of private physicians, but by just 41 percent of the private midwives. When it comes to adult curative care, the differences between *puskesmas* and private physicians are smaller; nurses compare more favorably, and midwives less favorably.

Table 5.6   Detailed Quality Scores on Prenatal, Child Curative, and Adult Curative Care Vignettes, by Clinical Setting, 2007

(percent)

Service	Puskesmas	Pustu	Private physician	Private midwife	Private nurse
Prenatal care					
Evaluate hypertensive disorders					
Ask about history of high blood pressure	44	34	13	39	5
Take blood pressure	89	80	28	89	18
Test urine protein	26	18	6	21	1
Ask about smoking habit	31	29	11	32	8
Take history and physical					
Ask about history of heart disease	27	21	10	27	4
Ask about history of diabetes	37	28	11	34	3
Ask about family history of illnesses	43	43	15	49	7
Take height measurements	72	59	17	63	6
Weigh patient	89	79	26	87	13
Measure uterine height	66	56	18	66	13
Assess whether high-risk pregnancy	20	16	8	21	3
Perform diagnostics and prevention					
Determine tetanus immune status	24	22	9	26	4
Test for STI	1	0	1	1	0
Test hemoglobin levels	72	46	17	55	8
Advise on nutrition	91	80	26	91	18
Give iron-folate	42	31	12	35	4
Establish case management system					
Date the pregnancy	24	19	5	26	4
Plan for delivery	24	18	6	24	3
Plan for follow-up visits	57	44	14	58	6
Adult curative care (respiratory)					
Take history and physical					
Ask about duration of illness	97	93	94	61	92
Ask about previous respiratory illnesses	20	11	22	8	13
Ask about blood in cough	54	42	64	30	43

(continued)

Table 5.6   Detailed Quality Scores on Prenatal, Child Curative, and Adult Curative Care Vignettes, by Clinical Setting, 2007 (continued)
(percent)

Service	Puskesmas	Pustu	Private physician	Private midwife	Private nurse
Ask about color of sputum	51	39	57	36	37
Ask about chest pain	39	31	46	24	33
Conduct physical and sputum					
Take temperature	75	77	72	53	71
Listen to respiration	71	65	68	44	60
Examine ears	34	23	41	12	16
Assess chest indrawing	40	31	40	20	27
Assess for cyanosis	76	65	78	47	65
Test sputum	75	68	61	38	63
Child curative care (diarrhea)					
Take history and physical					
Ask about duration of illness	86	89	83	73	72
Ask about frequency of illness	93	91	84	78	75
Ask about appearance of stools or vomit	54	33	55	34	34
Ask about blood in stools	42	28	43	26	22
Ask about fever	58	55	54	46	45
Conduct physical					
Take temperature	75	73	72	66	59
Check for sunken fontanelles	61	46	60	44	42
Check skin turgor	78	75	72	69	64
Take pulse	52	44	57	42	42
Check alertness	75	66	72	63	54
Provide care and advice					
Administer oral rehydration fluids	79	70	74	41	66
Recommend when to return if worse	35	25	34	25	23

Source: IFLS 2007, http://www.rand.org/labor/FLS/IFLS.

In sum, the more detailed analysis shows that prenatal care diagnostic and treatment abilities are higher at *puskesmas*, but adult and child curative care diagnostic and treatment ability scores are higher for private physicians. There is logic to this finding, particularly given the emphasis of public policy on maternal health and the fact that the Ministry of

Health and subnational governments provide more training to *puskesmas* providers. The core business of private practitioners, except for midwives, is child and adult curative care. Private midwives' scores are very similar to those of *puskesmas* on prenatal care but are less favorable on child and adult care.

For the different vignettes, the competency scores of public and private health providers were ranked into five quintiles (table 5.7). No major differences appear in average quintile vignette scores between public and private providers. For all quintiles, average scores improved over time. Even for the highest quintiles, however, average scores across vignettes are above 90 percent only for child curative care. Therefore, despite the improvements, the overall level of diagnostic and treatment ability of all health providers in Indonesia remains low. All health workers are expected to respond 100 percent correctly on basic standards.

Table 5.7   Competence Distribution of Public and Private Health Care Providers—Scores on Vignettes Measuring Diagnostic and Treatment Abilities
(*percent*)

Competence quintile	1997			2007		
	Prenatal care	Child curative care	Adult curative care	Prenatal care	Child curative care	Adult curative care
Public						
1st quintile (least competent)	18.6	31.1	20.9	27.6	43.8	30.7
2nd quintile	34.8	46.7	41.3	40.1	58.3	50.0
3rd quintile	44.6	58.3	54.5	47.4	66.7	63.6
4th quintile	55.5	69.6	68.2	53.9	79.0	72.7
5th quintile (most competent)	70.1	85.6	81.8	67.8	93.8	81.8
Private						
1st quintile (least competent)	17.0	26.6	22.5	24.9	29.9	29.5
2nd quintile	31.4	47.0	36.4	36.8	49.4	45.5
3rd quintile	44.4	58.3	50.8	45.0	63.6	54.5
4th quintile	55.5	69.8	63.6	55.1	77.0	68.0
5th quintile (most competent)	69.5	86.6	74.2	65.7	94.1	83.5

Source: IFLS 2007, http://www.rand.org/labor/FLS/IFLS.

Quality and In-Service Training

The findings described above are most likely related to the quality of preservice and in-service training. Previous studies have shown that such training is lagging in Indonesia, especially for nurses and midwives (Hennessy et al. 2006; World Bank 2008). It seems apparent that educational institutions and their regulatory framework need to be strengthened. At present, the regulatory framework governing the quality of these institutions is weak. Of particular concern is the rapid growth of new schools without a proper credentialing process. Although reforms and increased investment to address the quality of health professional institutions are ongoing, results in the form of increased quality cannot be expected in the short term.[6] Not only is preservice training lagging, but internships to help students obtain practical clinical skills are in short supply and of poor quality.

Most of the analysis in this chapter controls for a number of background factors, such as health providers' age, and village fixed effects; however, experience and training were not directly included. Although it is likely that age is picking up a substantial part of the effect that experience (years) generates, some further analysis was performed to assess the possible contribution of training. To assess the correlation between diagnostic ability and training that health workers and providers have previously received, only IFLS 2007 survey data were used for multivariate analyses, as that was the only wave that included information on training. Diagnostic ability was measured as described above, and estimated models controlled for type of provider, work experience, and district fixed effects.

The correlation between training and the quality of care varied widely across vignettes (table 5.8). No correlation seemed to exist between training and quality of prenatal care. That may be explained by the fact that in-service training in maternal health normally focuses on birth delivery skills and not necessarily on prenatal care. For child curative care, a significant positive correlation appeared between the raw score on the child curative care vignette and receipt of training for acute respiratory, malaria, nutrition, and prenatal care. A significant positive correlation was also observed between the adult curative care score and receipt of the following types of training: diagnostic algorithm, respiratory disease, and antibiotics for respiratory disease (for the detailed analysis, see appendix 5 under the heading The Correlations between Training and Experience and Health Provider Knowledge).

Table 5.8   Types of Training and Experience with a Positive Effect on Provider Quality Shown by Vignette Scores

Diagnostic vignette	Has positive effect on raw score	Has positive effect on ability to score above average
Prenatal care	No training correlations	Years of experience
Child curative care	Acute respiratory infections	—
	Malaria	
Adult curative care	Diagnostic algorithm	—
	Respiratory disease	

Source: IFLS 2007, http://www.rand.org/labor/FLS/IFLS.

Note: This table summarizes the types of training that had significant positive correlation with diagnostic vignette scores in the models developed and presented in appendix 5, tables A5.3 to A5.5. The types of training include training that the health worker received in the last 12 months in diagnostic algorithm for adult diseases, noncommunicable diseases, respiratory diseases, antibiotics for respiratory diseases (for adult curative care), child immunization, treatment for acute respiratory infection, treatment of diarrhea, treatment of malaria, nutrition, HIV transmission in pregnancy, prenatal care (for child curative care), safe delivery, high-risk pregnancy, assistance during labor, HIV in pregnancy, obstetrical emergency, and family planning (for prenatal care). — = no effect.

Changes in Quality and Growth of the Private Sector

Growth in the number of private practices might bring about either improvements or deterioration in the average quality of medical services available in a community. On the one hand, without licensing and standards, more private health care providers who are poorly trained or low skilled may lead to a decline in average quality. On the other hand, if new private practices are staffed by providers with above-average skills and diagnostic abilities, they will contribute directly to an improvement in average quality. Higher-quality private practices may also raise quality indirectly if providers in the public *puskesmas* respond positively to competition from private providers. Correlations between growth in private health services and overall diagnostic and treatment ability are presented in table 5.9. The correlations are from multivariate analyses examining changes in diagnostic ability while controlling for legacy effects of past ability, changes in the socioeconomic characteristics of the community, and changes in demand for health care.[7]

The results of the analysis presented in table 5.9 suggest several consistent messages:

First, increase in the number of private sector physicians per 100,000 population is associated with improvement in the average diagnostic ability of all facilities. The change in prenatal care, child curative care, and adult curative care scores from diagnostic and treatment vignettes are all positively correlated with changes in the number of private physician

Table 5.9   Effect of an Increase in Private Practices on Diagnostic Ability of Health Care Providers

	Sample	
Population	All facilities	Public facilities
Prenatal vignette score		
Change in private physicians	0.057**	0.021
per 100,000 population	(0.025)	(0.026)
Change in private midwife	–0.001	–0.001
practices per 100,000 population	(0.001)	(0.014)
Child curative care vignette score		
Change in private physicians	0.069**	0.023
per 100,000 population	(0.031)	(0.037)
Change in private midwife	–0.018	–0.002
practices per 100,000 population	(0.027)	(0.025)

Source: Calculated by authors from IFLS, http://www.rand.org/labor/FLS/IFLS, and PODES (http://www.rand.org/labor/bps/podes/) data.

Note: This table shows the change in prenatal and child curative care z-scores associated with changes in numbers of physician and midwife practices per 100,000 population. The eight coefficients estimated in the table summarize results from four models estimated in appendix 5, tables A5.1 and A5.2. Column 1 summarizes the effects of expanding private sector provision on average diagnostic ability (measured as z-scores of community average score) within an enumeration area and uses coefficients from Model 4 of the upper panel in tables A5.1 and A5.2. Column 2 summarizes the effect of private sector expansion on average diagnostic ability in public facilities and uses coefficients from Model 4 of the lower panel in tables A5.1 and A5.2. Standard errors of the estimated effect are shown in parentheses. For more information on the models estimated, including other characteristics included as controls, please see the discussion in appendix 5, and for the full set of estimation results, see tables A5.1 and A5.2. *** indicates significance at the 1 percent level, ** at 5 percent, and * at 10 percent.

practices in the community. These relationships are statistically significant for prenatal and child curative care. It is important to note that an increase in the number of private sector physicians is associated with improvements in average diagnostic and treatment ability in the community, whether by a physician, midwife, or nurse. Although it is difficult to measure, it is possible that lower-level staff (nurses) may learn from more educated staff (physicians) and thereby improve their own service quality.

Second, the analysis gives no evidence that dual practice opportunities lead to decline in the diagnostic and treatment ability of health care workers in the *puskesmas*.[8] One worry regarding the growth in private practices is that it may have a detrimental effect on the quality of care in the *puskesmas* if physicians based in the *puskesmas* believe they can earn substantially higher incomes through operating their own private practices. Quality in the *puskesmas* may deteriorate if physicians are simply not available. This study found that the diagnostic ability of the health care providers available in the *puskesmas* did not deteriorate with the growth of the private sector. This finding is positive in particular because responses to the vignettes reflect the ability of *puskesmas* staff who were present when survey administrators arrived unannounced. At the same time, further study of physician time use in public and private services is important for a more complete understanding of the costs and benefits of dual practice in Indonesia. It is especially important because a large percentage of the government's public health expenditures covers the salaries of public providers. It should also be kept in mind that although the quality of health personnel, as measured by these vignettes, is an important dimension of care, other dimensions of quality are also important, including effort of the provider, effectiveness, efficiency, and interpersonal relations, none of which is captured by the vignette score.

Third, given the existence of policies that have led to a vast expansion in the number of private sector midwives, it is interesting that increasing the number of midwives per 100,000 people is not correlated with improvements in quality. Still, the absence of a positive association between vignette scores and number of midwives should not be interpreted as evidence that the increased number of midwives has not improved access to care or health outcomes.[9] The lack of an association could derive from the fact that the increases in number of midwives were similar across communities within regions, so that after the multivariate analysis controls for regional growth in midwife practices, a separate midwife effect cannot be observed.

Notes

1. See the section Data and Methodology, in chapter 1, for caveats in using vignettes to measure quality.

2. An important note of caution: the answers demonstrate knowledge, not practice.

3. The normalized score, or z-score, is the raw score, minus average raw score, divided by the standard deviation of the raw score.

4. For the 2007 IFLS, the following types of respondents were interviewed: for the prenatal care vignette, general practitioners (5 percent), midwives (90 percent), paramedics (5 percent); for the child curative care vignette, general practitioners (36 percent), midwives (41 percent), nurses (21 percent), and paramedics (2 percent); for adult curative care, general practitioners (55 percent), midwives (16 percent), nurses (25 percent), and paramedics (2 percent).

5. As shown, for the prenatal care vignette, the midwife at the *puskesmas* was the respondent questioned in 90 percent of the interviews. Given that most

midwives provide both public and private services, it is no surprise that there is little difference in quality between the two providers.

6. The World Bank cofinances the Health Professional Education Quality project, managed by the Directorate General for Higher Education at the Indonesian Ministry of National Education, which aims to strengthen the quality assurance policies governing the education of health professionals in Indonesia by (a) rationalizing accreditation of public and private health professional training institutions and ensuring that it is competency focused; (b) developing national competency standards and testing procedures for certification and licensing of health professionals; and (c) building institutional capacity to employ results-based grants to encourage the use of accreditation and certification standards in the development of medical school quality.

7. Appendix 5 contains a discussion of the methodological approach; an expanded set of results appears in appendix 5 tables A5.1 and A5.2.

8. A negative and significant coefficient on change in number of physician practices per 100,000 could be driven by the fact that physicians with side practices were not in their public health clinic offices at the time that enumerators showed up.

9. Other research has raised questions about whether increases in the number of midwives have led to improved health outcomes. The correlation between number of midwives and maternal deaths was studied in two districts of Banten province in 2006. Researchers found no differences in the number of maternal deaths in villages with higher numbers of midwives (Ronsmans et al. 2009). Yet there are Frankenberg-Thomas papers that suggest a positive effect of midwives on maternal and child health (Frankenberg and Thomas 2001).

References

Barber, S. L., P. J. Gertler, and P. Harimurti. 2007a. "Differences in Access to High-Quality Outpatient Care in Indonesia." *Health Affairs* 26 (3): w352–66.

———. 2007b. "The Contribution of Human Resources for Health to the Quality of Care in Indonesia." *Health Affairs* 26 (3): w367–79.

BPS (*Badan Pusat Statistik* [Indonesia Statistics Bureau]), National Family Planning Coordinating Board, Ministry of Health, and Macro International. 2008. *Demographic and Health Survey 2007.* Calverton, Maryland, USA: BPS and Macro International. http://demografi.bps.go.id/versi2/index.php.

Frankenberg, E., and D. Thomas. 2001. "Women's Health and Pregnancy Outcomes: Do Services Make a Difference?" *Demography* 38 (2): 253–65.

Hennessy, D., C. Hicks, A. Hilan, and Y. Kawonal. 2006. "The Training and Development Needs of Nurses in Indonesia." Paper 3 of 3. *Human Resources for Health* 4: 10. http://www.human-resources-health/content/4/1/10.

Ronsmans, C., S. Scott, S. N. Qomariyah, E. Achadi, D. Braunholtz, T. Marshall, E. Pambudi, K. H. Witten, and W. J. Graham. 2009. "Professional Assistance during Birth and Maternal Mortality in Two Indonesian Districts." *Bulletin of the World Health Organization 2009* 87: 416–23.

Thomas, D., E. Frankenberg, J. Friedman, J.-P. Habicht, C. McKelvey, N. Jones, G. Pelto, B. Sikoki, C. Sumantri, and W. Suriastini. 2007. "Iron Supplementation, Iron Deficient Anemia, and Hemoglobinopathies: Evidence from Older Adults in Rural Indonesia." Unpublished manuscript, University of California, Los Angeles.

World Bank. 2008. *Investing in Indonesia's Health: Challenges and Opportunities for Future Public Spending. Health Public Expenditure Review 2008.* Jakarta: World Bank.

CHAPTER 6

Discussion and Policy Suggestions

The Indonesia Family Life Survey (IFLS) database offers a unique opportunity to address the questions that the study raised about the supply and quality of health providers and the use of health services, as it allows comparisons over time and includes quality measures. Matching the IFLS with the PODES survey (*Potensi Desa*, or Survey of Village Potential) further makes it possible to analyze changes in the quantity of health providers and changes in quality, as well as the effects of the growth of the private health workforce in Indonesia. Although it should be kept in mind that the IFLS does not include most of the eastern Indonesian provinces, it covers 85 percent of the Indonesian population.

The quality measures used in the study relate to structural quality at the facility level (that is, the availability of adequate supplies and infrastructure) and diagnostic and treatment ability. Diagnostic and treatment abilities were measured through health workers' responses to vignette questions representing three types of care—prenatal, child curative, and adult curative. The questions measured knowledge, not effort, an important distinction to keep in mind while interpreting the results.

This chapter sets out suggestions for policy discussion and for further research and analysis. Suggestions flowing directly from the evidence presented in this study will be discussed. These stem from findings on the supply, distribution, and quality of the health workforce. Where relevant, related policy suggestions, stemming from previous work on the health workforce, and policies affecting health workers and their deployment and services are included to permit a more comprehensive set of suggestions to Indonesian stakeholders. Finally, policy areas where further research or analysis is necessary are briefly discussed. These are important policy areas that should not be disregarded but for which specific suggestions for reform cannot yet be provided. Overall, the following policy recommendations are meant to stimulate debate and discussion among Indonesian policy makers and academics and are not intended to be prescriptions.

Key Findings on Quantity and Distribution

Since the late 1990s, the supply of health services in urban, rural, and remote areas has grown, especially as a result of the increase in the provision of private services by public providers. Although this "dual practice" has increased overall access to services, it has not contributed to a more equitable distribution across regions. Since 1996, *puskesmas* have had, on average, more physicians. At the same time, however, more *puskesmas* lack physicians, especially ones in rural areas.

The distribution of general practitioners remains a serious concern, with only 6 per 100,000 population in rural areas and 36 per 100,000 in urban areas. The government's policies to improve the distribution of health workers do not appear to have been entirely successful, except for midwives. More recently, the shortening of the mandatory period of service in remote areas from three years to six months appears to have induced more physicians to take up remote area assignments.

Growth in the number of private practices in communities is associated with a significant increase in use of health facilities by poorer members of the community. The poor are more likely to use the public *puskesmas* as the private sector grows. This suggests that the increase in supply of health service providers reduces congestion costs in the public *puskesmas*, while also sorting more affluent members of the community to private practices.

One of the key barriers limiting access to health services is financial: people tend not to seek care out of fear they will not be able to afford it. When financial barriers are removed, one would expect an increase in utilization. The *Askeskin/Jamkesmas* (Health Insurance for the Poor) program is intended to remove financial barriers and allow poor people better access to health services. The IFLS database allowed analysis of changes in utilization by those who have *Askeskin/Jamkesmas* insurance, which showed that utilization by individuals from the poorest 20 percent of households increased by 2.8 percent after the *Askeskin/Jamkesmas* program commenced. Use by individuals in the next-poorest quintile of the local per capita expenditure distribution rose by 2.9 percent.[1] Much of the change in utilization from 1997 to 2007 may thus be associated with access to *Askeskin/Jamkesmas*. Use of health care by more affluent households, in the 4th quintile of the per capita expenditure distribution, also increased.[2]

Policy Suggestions on Quantity and Distribution

- Monitoring and evaluating current deployment policy appear crucial to ascertain whether it is an effective long-term strategy for maintaining quality health workers in remote areas. The current government's deployment policy of mandatory six-month service in a remote area, combined with financial and nonfinancial incentives, appears to have had a positive effect in the short term. Although short periods in a location may be sufficient for improving access to curative care, promotive and preventive care requires a more stable presence in one location, if providers are to understand the particular context and know patients.

- In addition to evaluation of the current policy of reduced mandatory service, it is highly recommended that the government of Indonesia continue to develop and experiment with other incentive schemes to improve deployment and ensure that quality health services are available in rural and remote areas for the long term. Appendix 6 provides a listing of various types of financial and nonfinancial incentives as an illustration of possibilities.[3] Gadjah Mada University is conducting some promising initial experiments using nonfinancial incentives—such as creating a more appealing working environment by bringing together teams with a mix of skills—which merit more attention and evaluation. Recently, attention in the international literature has turned toward creating a "rural pipeline" by focusing on recruitment from rural areas, for example, creating increased interest in the health professions in secondary schools and developing specific rural curriculums in health professional schools. Fostering experiments and pilots with these new developments is recommended.

- Planning and budgeting should include consideration of the private health sector to ensure more optimal use of existing resources. This could consist of contracting out services and promoting health insurance schemes that allow for equalization of reimbursement rates for public and private providers. The private health sector provides about one-half of all health services in Indonesia and continues to grow.

- For improvement of planning and needs-based licensing processes, it is recommended that a more comprehensive set of data be collected on who works where, both publicly and privately. At present, data are fragmented and incomplete. The current process, in which local governments license new private health practices, is inadequate and is not based on need; nor does it sufficiently take existing health care resources into account. Linking planning with overall civil service reforms is also imperative.

- A more thorough analysis of the hours health care providers spend in public and in private facilities and of the cost-effectiveness of allowing dual practice is needed to gain a better understanding of the impact of dual practice and to adapt policy where necessary. Indonesia's impressive gains in access to health services are explained in part by dual practice. Coupled with removal of financial barriers, dual practice has increased utilization both of public facilities, *puskesmas* and *pustu*, and of private physicians, midwives, and nurses. Although the study found no evidence that dual practice has a negative impact on the knowledge of health care providers at the *puskesmas*, this study cannot comment on other important dimensions of the quality of services, such as effort and time spent with patients. Analysis of physicians' knowledge and use of time in public and private practice would provide a more complete picture of whether dual practice opportunities have a negative impact on the quality of care available in the *puskesmas*.

- More understanding is needed about the impact of the sorting of patients in which the poor make more use of public services while the more affluent seek care at private facilities. The initial indication is that the existence of dual practice has contributed to the sorting of patients. This may have a positive impact on efficiency, as long as the nonpoor continue to support the public system. Questions regarding efficiency gains from the existence of higher-priced private options, as well as implications for quality in both public and private sectors, require further study. The data do not, however, allow an analysis of providers' hours and level of effort spent in providing public and private services.

- A review is highly recommended of the use of public funds and the efforts expended toward ensuring an adequate supply of health workers in underserved areas and for the poorest per capita expenditure quintiles. Use of public services has decreased substantially since the 1997–98 economic and financial crisis, and although some increases have occurred since 2000, it remains far below earlier levels. Instead, utilization of private services, especially those of private midwives and nurses, has increased. A large part of public spending goes to operate public facilities that have seen declining utilization rates, especially by richer quintiles, in places where private services are available. Moreover, the continuing one-size-fits-all service delivery strategy in Indonesia is inadequate, as it does not take into account the diversity across the country's regions.

- Indonesia should consider allowing a privileging of certain interventions by nurses and midwives in rural and remote areas. Nurses and midwives continue to be among the primary providers of health services for the poor in remote and rural areas. As shown by the analysis of changes in utilization, when they are ill, most people now seek treatment from nurses and midwives. Yet the low level of quality of nurses providing private services is alarming and needs urgent attention.

- The overall staffing plans in the health sector need to be adapted to local needs and to changes in policies and should take the ongoing demographic, epidemiological, and nutritional transitions into account. For example, in areas where many physicians in private practice are providing curative care, the lack of a physician in a *puskesmas* may not be of concern, as long as the poor have access to private physicians as well. Such an arrangement could be achieved through changing the reimbursement policies of *Askeskin/Jamkesmas* to include care by private physicians.

- The demographic, epidemiological, and nutritional transitions that are occurring in Indonesia will require adaptations in the skills mix, number, and distribution of health workers and should be taken into account when developing the reforms suggested here.

Key Findings Regarding Quality

The overall quality of health services provided, as measured by the diagnostic and treatment ability of the main health care providers—general practitioners, midwives, and nurses—improved between 1997 and 2007. Positive trends are seen among midwives in prenatal care and among general practitioners in adult care. However, considering the efforts to improve training that were implemented during the period, the increase is marginal. A large proportion of providers do not meet the standards set for quality health services. It appears that current education requirements for health professionals and the regulatory process governing the quality of health professional education are inadequate. Quality control over providers is also insufficient to guarantee high-quality health services.

The correlation between provider training and the quality of care varied widely across vignettes. Although no correlation appeared between training and the quality of prenatal care, a positive correlation was seen between child curative care vignette scores and provider training. A positive correlation was seen between adult curative care score and receipt of the training in diagnostic algorithm, respiratory disease, and antibiotics for respiratory disease.

Increasing the number of private sector physicians per 100,000 population is associated with improvement in the average diagnostic ability of all facilities. Improvements in prenatal care, child curative care, and adult curative care scores on the diagnostic and treatment vignettes are all positively correlated with changes in the number of private physician practices in the community. The relationships are statistically significant for prenatal and child curative care.

There is no evidence that dual practice opportunities have led to a decline in the diagnostic and treatment ability of health care workers in the *puskesmas*.[4] Although this is a positive finding, further study of physicians' use of their time in public and private services is important for a more complete understanding of the costs and benefits of dual practice in Indonesia. This is especially important because a large percentage of public health salary spending goes to pay the salaries of public providers.

Vignettes measure knowledge, not effort. It should be kept in mind that although quality of health personnel, as measured by the vignettes, is an important dimension of care, other dimensions of quality are also important. They include effort of the provider, effectiveness, efficiency, and interpersonal relations, none of which is captured by the vignette score.

As a footnote to the findings of this analysis, Sumatra appears to be lagging the other regions in improvements in both the quantity and quality of health services. This trend is peculiar to the health sector. Other social sectors, such as education and economic development, do not exhibit this pattern. No explanation for this finding is apparent.

Policy Suggestions Regarding Quality

- For Indonesia to improve the quality of service provision, the regulatory framework that governs the providers and the quality of their training needs urgent attention. Experimentation and pilot programs with different provider payment mechanisms are highly recommended. Much of the improvement in quality of service provision is embedded in two parts of the health system: the regulatory framework and provider payment incentives. The proliferation of private health care providers without adequate oversight of the quality of services they provide, along with the marginal improvement in health service provision despite increased attention to training for providers, warrants revisiting current policies.

    Specific actions include (a) establishing competency and education standards and a regulatory body for nurses and midwives, (b) rationalizing accreditation of public and private health professional training institutions and ensuring that it is competency focused, and (c) encouraging the professional associations to improve the continuing education program and link it to licensing.

- Following those measures, a concrete step that the government could consider is limiting the recruitment of doctors as civil servants to those who have been certified according to national standards. Such a policy will ensure the efficient use of public resources, as well as motivate health providers to obtain accreditation and certification. Many health providers are graduating from schools that are not accredited, or are insufficiently accredited, and the certification process is lacking. An urgent need also exists to better control the establishment of new schools and link that establishment to the accreditation system.

- The certification of physicians, nurses, and midwives should be strengthened to measure skills, not only knowledge, as is currently the practice. As accreditation and certification standards and processes for facilities are improved, a needs-based master plan covering the whole country, both the public and the private sector, could be developed, including both facilities and manpower. Private sector involvement in medical and paramedical education also warrants strong public sector oversight to ensure quality of services.

Further Research Options: Provider Payment Methods

Indonesia has initiated some interesting pilots and experiments with provider payment methods, such as the introduction of diagnosis-related groups and global budgeting at the hospital level, but much more could be done. The move toward universal health insurance coverage could be used to further experiment with, and modernize, provider payment methods in several ways:

- Developing payment systems based on performance that reflect the efficient costs of service provision and treat public and private sector providers similarly.
- Evaluating and continuing to pilot results-based financing systems, such as output-based payments, global budgets for hospitals, and per diem case-based diagnosis-related groups for facilities and individual providers to increase efficiency and quality.
- Experimenting with nonmonetary incentives for all providers, especially midwives, including better career opportunities, merit-based career management, and improved in-kind benefits (such as housing and education), to encourage deployment to remote areas.

Notes

1. As is illustrated by findings from Model 3; see appendix 4, table A4.1.
2. Explicit analyses of the *Askeskin/Jamkesmas* program were performed but are not included in this book. A full analysis of the effects of the program will be produced in a separate research publication.
3. For guidance on developing an incentive package, see *Guidelines: Incentives for Health Professionals*, 2008, at http://www.who.int/workforcealliance/documents/Incentives_Guidelines%20EN.pdf.
4. A negative and significant coefficient on change in number of physician practices per 100,000 people could be driven by the fact that physicians with side practices were not in their public health clinic offices at the time that enumerators showed up.

Data Sources

The primary data source that is used for analyses in this study is the Indonesia Family Life Survey (IFLS). For some questions, information from the Survey of Village Potential (*Potensi Desa*, or PODES) is merged with IFLS. Supplementary analyses from the nationally representative surveys called the *Susenas* are used to examine trends over time.

The IFLS data collected in 1993, 1997, 2000, and 2007–08 include facility surveys, with information on staff in both public and private facilities. Provider data are matched to individual patients (and potential patients) within enumeration areas. Since the survey follows the same households and villages over time, it can provide a useful opportunity to examine changes that have occurred with the growth of dual practice and the private sector. The *Susenas* is a household survey with some questions about illness and health care utilization, but the types of self-reports it uses suffer from notorious sources of bias. The IFLS 2007 data include vignettes that can be used to construct measures of the quality of the practical, treatment-oriented knowledge that health care providers possess. Quality measures constructed from vignettes are independent of the respondents' formal titles.

Every four years the *Susenas* contains a special health module that includes health status questions and information on health utilization, as well as information on access to *Askeskin/Jamkesmas* insurance.[1] The *Susenas* survey rounds can be merged with the village infrastructure survey, PODES, which contains questions about health providers in the village. From PODES, one can determine the number of public and private health providers (physicians, nurses, and midwives) living in the village, and these can be used to construct a proxy variable for the size of the local private sector.[2]

Notes

1. In 2007, the Ministry of Health (MoH) took over implementation of the health module that was formerly conducted every three years as part of the *Susenas* survey. The health survey conducted by MoH is called Riskesdas, *riset kesehatan dasar* (or basic health research).

2. It should be cautioned that measures of self-reported health status, such as those found in the *Susenas*, are problematic as indicators for behavioral studies because they are typically confounded with unobserved socioeconomic characteristics and unobserved prior health care utilization.

Definitions of Health Facilities and Providers

Health Facilities

Health facility	Description	Public or private
Public hospital (*rumah sakit umum daerah* [RSUD])	Public hospital located at the district level	Public
Private hospital (*rumah sakit umum swasta* [RSUS])	Private hospital located at the district level; national and provincial government enterprises, police, defense forces	Private
Private hospital for women and children (*rumah sakit ibu dan anak* [RSIA])	Private hospital for women and children located in the district	Private
Maternity clinic (*rumah sakit bersalin* [RSB])	Private women's hospital located in the district	Private
Private maternity clinic (*rumah bersalin* [RB])	Private maternity clinics with more than two beds	Private
Community health center (*pusat kesehatan masyarakat*)	Public health center; in general, they are located at the subdistrict level.	Public
Auxiliary health center (*pustu*)	Public health subcenter; in general, they are located at the subdistrict level, usually in the village.	Public
Village midwife (*bidan di desa* [BDD]/ *pondok bersalin desa* [polindes])	A BDD is a village midwife who receives a government salary but may charge for the services she provides and retain the fees. Although the village midwife theoretically lives in the village (*desa*), there are reports that in many villages she lives elsewhere, maybe in a nearby urban area. The services provided by the BDD may be offered in a room in her house or in a structure that is the property of, and was built by, the village government (*polindes*). In the *polindes*, the services are provided by the village midwife, who charges for the services and retains the fees.	Private

Treatment clinic (*balai pengobatan* [BPI])	Before the advent of the health center, many private and public treatment clinics existed. As the health center was developed, the public treatment clinics were incorporated into the health centers, with the result that only the private *balai pengobatan* remained. Although they have been ignored by the government and donors, they remain a significant source of treatment, especially in urban areas. They are licensed by the local government and must have a doctor as the supervisor. In practice, most of the doctors named as supervisor seldom visit, and nurses and some midwives provide most of the health care unsupervised.	Private
Doctor, private practice (*dokter praktek swasta* [DPS] *murni*)	A doctor whose primary professional activity is private practice and who does not receive a salary from the government	Private
Nurse, private practice (*perawat praktek swasta* [PPS] *murni*)	A nurse whose primary professional activity is private practice and who does not receive a salary from the government	Private
Midwife, private practice (*bidan praktek swasta* [BPS] *murni*)	A midwife whose primary professional activity is private practice and who does not receive a salary from the government	Private

Health Service Providers

Provider	Description
Doctor (*dokter*)	Graduate of an Indonesian medical school licensed by the government
Nurse (*perawat*)	Graduate of 1. a *sekolah perawat kesehatan* (SPK); students enter at the end of junior high school, and the SPK training is regarded as equivalent to senior high school; or 2. an *akademi perawatan*, which students enter at the end of senior high school; or 3. *fakultas ilmu keperawatan*, a university-level course at the first degree level; a small number are second degree–level graduates as well. All these institutions must be licensed by the government.

(continued)

Health Service Providers *(continued)*

Provider	Description
Midwife (*bidan*)	Graduate of 1. *sekolah bidan* (SB), which students enter at the end of junior high school; this training is regarded as equivalent to senior high school; or 2. *program pendidikan bidan* (PPB); entrants to this one-year program have an SPK nursing qualification; or 3. *akademi kebidanan (akbid)*, which students enter at the end of senior high school. Originally, midwives were trained as SB until that program was closed in 1984. After five years of no training of midwives, the government started training again in 1989 through the PPB village midwives program. The PPB was closed in 1998 and was replaced by the *akbid* program.

Source: Adapted from P. F. Heywood and N. P. Harahap, "Human Resources for Health at the District Level in Indonesia: The Smoke and Mirrors of Decentralization," *Human Resources for Health*, 2009, 7:6.

Note: A health facility is defined as a physical structure, varying from a large complex of buildings to a single room in a house, from which health services are offered by a doctor, nurse, or midwife.

Convergence in Quality

The analysis summarized in table 5.3 (chapter 5) demonstrates that although significant positive changes in quality have occurred, these changes are very minor. More thorough analysis of how the changes took place within groups and across regions reveals that there is more to the story than simple small improvements.

Figure A3.1 shows the 10-year change in community average scores for each of the diagnostic vignettes (prenatal care, child curative care, and adult curative care), plotted against the initial 1997 raw score. The declining slope of the relationship between initial score and change in score suggests convergence in the quality of care across communities: communities with low initial scores experienced the sharpest increases in quality, and communities with higher average scores saw slower increases, or even decreases, in scores over the 10 year period.

That a number of communities with high average scores on diagnostic vignettes in 1997 experienced declines by 2007 may result from two processes. First, and less worrisome, the average in each community is calculated from a subset of health care providers that includes the public health center (*puskesmas*) and a random sample of other providers used by members of the community. Apart from the *puskesmas*, there is no guarantee that the same facilities were sampled in 1997 and

Figure A3.1   Evidence of Convergence in Quality: Change in Community Average Vignette Scores, 1997–2007

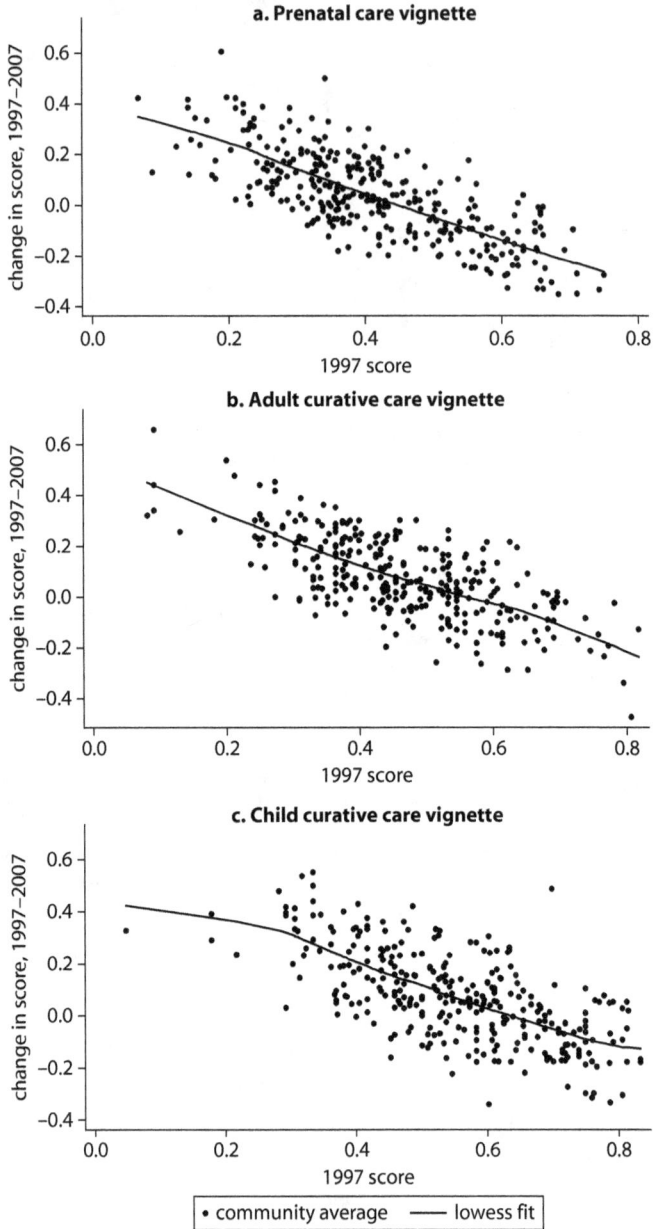

Source: IFLS 1997, 2007, http://www.rand.org/labor/FLS/IFLS.

in 2007, and so some of the apparent decline may reflect the inclusion of lower-quality providers in 2007. In this case, the apparent decline in quality may simply reflect randomness in providers sampled in each of the two survey rounds. Average diagnostic ability in the community is measured with error in each period because not all providers are included in the sample, and mean reversion may explain some of the apparent convergence.

Another explanation for this pattern, however, would be that it is difficult to retain high-quality health providers in community health clinics. In this case, the observed declines in quality could be caused by personnel changes over the previous 10 years. Communities with health care providers who scored particularly well on diagnostic vignettes in 1997 were not able to retain or to attract health care providers of the same quality over the 10 year period. In this case, some convergence is driven by a process in which a community with providers at the high end of the quality distribution simply did not have the luck to have health providers of the same quality 10 years later.

Quality Convergence by Region

Differences in patterns of vignette score convergence are also observed across provinces. In figure A3.2, convergence processes are shown separately for Java and Bali, Sumatra, and Other Provinces for average scores on each of three diagnostic vignettes. On all three vignettes, an interesting difference is observed between those provinces outside of Java and Bali and of Sumatra. Among communities with average vignette scores below roughly 0.4 in 1997, the increase in scores was more pronounced over the 10-year period. This may reflect efforts to increase access to health care providers in more remote regions, such as the obligatory public placement policy with incentives for remote and rural area service.

In addition, distinct differences in convergence patterns across the different vignettes are observed. In Java and Bali, for example, we do not observe the same steep convergence at the high end of the vignette distribution for the child curative care vignette as we do for the prenatal care and adult curative care vignettes. Communities in Java and Bali that had health care providers with raw scores on child curative care vignettes above 0.6 did not see significant deterioration in scores. In Other Provinces, communities scoring high in 1997 saw a greater deterioration

Figure A3.2   Regional Differences in Quality Convergence: Change in Community Average Vignette Scores, 1997–2007

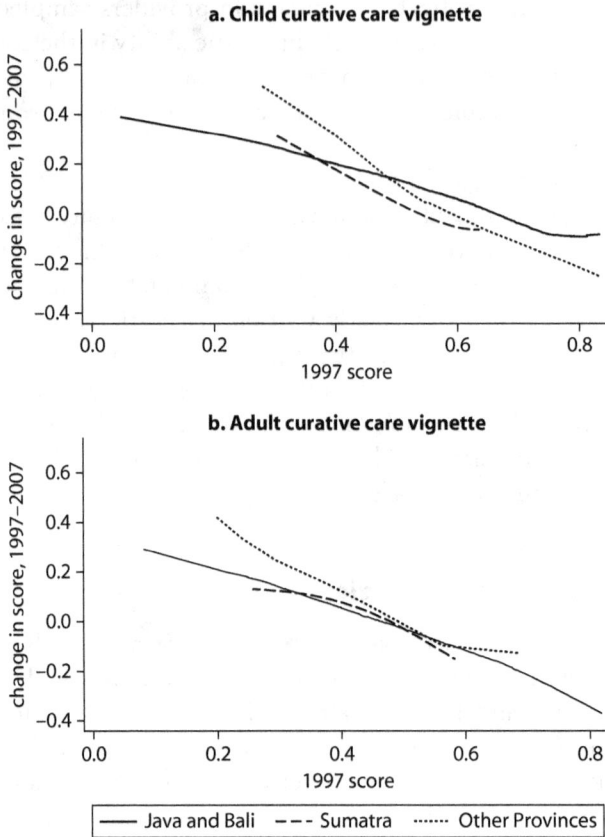

a. Child curative care vignette

b. Adult curative care vignette

Java and Bali   – – – Sumatra   ⋯⋯ Other Provinces

Source: IFLS 1997, 2007, http://www.rand.org/labor/FLS/IFLS.

in child curative care scores over 10 years. This may reflect greater difficulty in maintaining quality health personnel outside Java and Bali.

With respect to Sumatra, similar convergence patterns are observed across all three vignettes: the distribution of quality is much narrower in 1997. Communities with the lowest quality scores in 1997 do not have scores as low as the low-scoring communities in Java and Bali and Other Provinces, and at the other end of the distribution, high scores are not as high. Moreover, the highest-scoring communities in Sumatra, particularly for child curative care, did not experience as much deterioration in vignette scores as high-scoring communities in Java and Bali and Other Provinces.

Rural-Urban Differences in Quality Convergence

When one examines differences in convergence patterns across rural and urban areas, it is apparent that urban communities with low vignette scores in 1997 experienced greater improvement over 10 years than rural communities with similarly low scores. A rural community with a score of 20 percent saw its score on the prenatal care vignette increase by 20 points to 40 percent, while the increase for an urban community was from 30 percent to 50 percent. A similar gap exists for the child curative and adult curative care vignettes (figure A3.3). The larger magnitude of the increase in scores for urban communities probably reflects one of two phenomena: urban communities lacking personnel in 1997 may have found it easier to attract well-trained health care providers than rural areas, or more absenteeism may be occurring in rural area health facilities.

Differences in Quality Convergence by Socioeconomic Status

A final comparison examines convergence in vignette raw scores by community socioeconomic status. The study ranked communities by average per capita expenditure in 1997 and split the sample into three groups: an upper tercile with higher average consumption, a middle tercile, and a lower, poorer tercile. No significantly different convergence patterns appeared across villages of different socioeconomic status. Average convergence patterns are almost identical for prenatal care and child curative care vignettes while there is some evidence that poorer communities with low adult curative care vignette scores in 1997 saw somewhat less improvement than middle and upper terciles.

That little convergence by socioeconomic status was seen, compared to urban-rural status, may in part reflect the fact that health care providers are more willing to work in poorer communities than in rural and more remote communities. A physician may work in the health clinic of a poorer urban community and live elsewhere in the same city, but that may be more difficult in rural areas. More research is necessary to assess this possibility.

Figure A3.3   Rural-Urban Differences in Quality Convergence: Change in Community Average Vignette Scores, 1997–2007

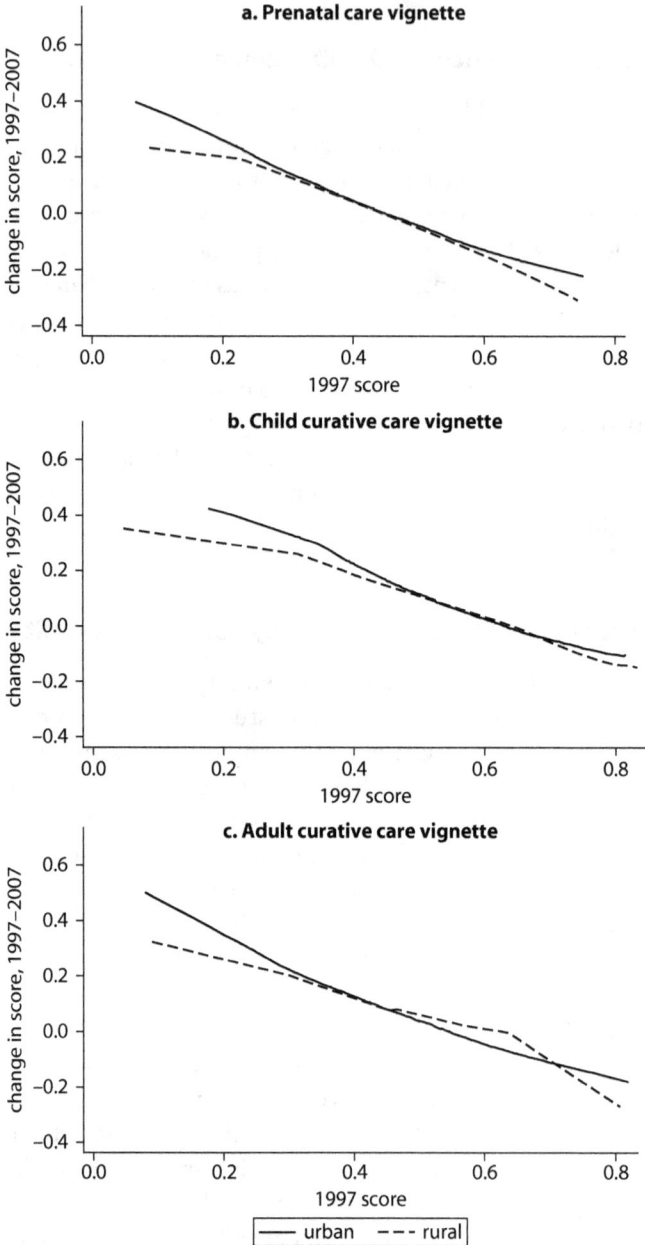

Private Health Care Providers and Utilization

The study examined changes in utilization patterns by socioeconomic status within communities, with attention to the role that growth in private sector provision of services may have played in changes in utilization. Within each enumeration area and for each year, the study first ranked households by average per capita expenditure and then recorded the household's quintile of the local expenditure distribution. These quintiles range from the poorest 20 percent to richest 20 percent within enumeration areas. In a base model, the correlation between relative socioeconomic status, or position within the distribution of per capita expenditure, and utilization patterns was first examined. To do this, a binary choice model was estimated in which the dependent variable, U, is equal to one if an individual utilized a health care provider when ill, and zero if not. Consider first the following base model:

$$U = \mathbf{PCE}_{it}'\beta + Y07 + \mathbf{X}_{it}'\alpha + d_{jt}^u + \mathbf{d}^d + \mu_{it},\qquad(1)$$

where $\mathbf{PCE}_{it}$ is a vector of five indicator variables indicating the per capita expenditure quintile of the household in which individual i resides in year t. We do not include a constant term, and thus coefficients on the five dummy variables composing $\mathbf{PCE}_{it}$ pick up the correlation between expenditure quintile and use of health services when ill. To isolate the correlation between socioeconomic status and utilization from other individual, community, and temporal effects, we include the following additional regressors: Y07 is a dummy equal to 1 in survey round 2007 and controls for changes in utilization patterns over the 10-year period; a vector of individual characteristics, X_{it}, which include education, gender, and a quartic in age (or age, age-squared, age-cubed, and age^4) to control for cohort effects; an indicator variable, d_{it}^u, which is equal to one if the community is classified as urban; a vector of district indicators, d^d, which control for time-invariant characteristics of the district in which an individual resides; and unexplained variation and error, μ_{it}.[1]

To examine effect of growth in the private sector at each quintile of the per capita expenditure distribution, the following was estimated:

$$U = PCE_{it}'\beta_1 + (PCE_{it} \bullet PRIV_{jt})\beta_2 + X_{it}'\alpha + d_{jt}^u + d^d + \mu_{it}. \qquad (2)$$

In this model, $PRIV_{jt}$ is the number of private sector practices per thousand[2] in community j at time t. The interaction of $PRIV_{jt}$ and the PCE_{it} dummy variables picks up differences in the association of private practice growth and health facility utilization at different points in the distribution of expenditures. The Survey of Village Potential (*Potensi Desa*, or PODES) conducted from 1996 and 2006 were used to determine the number of private practices in the local community. Other variables in this model are defined as in (2) above. The model is further expanded by splitting the private sector into doctors per thousand and midwives per thousand.

Table A4.1 first presents results using the entire sample. For the sake of parsimony, we present only the coefficients β_1 and β_2 and suppress those other coefficients that are not the object of the analysis. It is evident that growth of the private sector within a district is associated with expanded use of medical facilities by households in the poorer two quintiles of the per capita expenditure distribution.

Next, to distinguish between the effects of increasing private doctor and private midwife practices on utilization, we expand (2) above by using two interaction terms: private doctor practices per 1,000 population and midwife practices per 1,000 population, each interacted with indicator variables for quintile in the per capita expenditure distribution. The coefficients from these models are presented in Model 2 of table A4.1 below. It is immediately apparent that growth of private physician practices is more important for increasing the utilization of health facilities.

Although the model controls for fixed differences between urban and rural location and gender on utilization rates, it is also quite plausible

Table A4.1   How Does Utilization of Outpatient Services Vary with Socioeconomic Status and Access to Private Health Providers? (Full Sample)

Dependent variable: visited a health provider when ill (yes = 1)	Model 1		Model 2		
	Base	× Private	Base	× Private doctor	× Private midwife
Poorest 20 percent	−0.025	0.031***	−0.026	0.041**	0.025
of enumeration area	[0.017]	[0.012]	[0.017]	[0.017]	[0.017]
PCE at 2nd quintile	0.000	0.035***	−0.001	0.040**	0.031*
	[0.018]	[0.013]	[0.018]	[0.018]	[0.018]
PCE at 3rd quintile	0.024	−0.004	0.024	−0.01	0.003
	[0.017]	[0.013]	[0.017]	[0.017]	[0.018]
PCE at 4th quintile	0.035**	0.011	0.036**	−0.019	0.037**
	[0.017]	[0.013]	[0.017]	[0.018]	[0.018]
Richest 20 percent	0.071***	−0.022	0.071***	−0.041**	−0.004
	[0.018]	[0.014]	[0.018]	[0.020]	[0.019]
Observations		42,236			42,236
R-squared		0.254			0.254

Source: IFLS 1997, 2007, http://www.rand.org/labor/FLS/IFLS, estimated by authors.
Note: Standard errors in brackets. Other correlates include a year 2007 dummy, education (in years), age, age^2, age^3, age^4, gender, a dummy for urban community, and district fixed effects. PCE = per capita expenditure.
*** $p < 0.01$, ** $p < 0.05$, * $p < 0.10$.

that growth of the private sector may have different effects in different regions and across genders. For this reason, we next proceed to estimate (2) for four separate subsamples: urban male, urban female, rural male, and rural female. Results are shown in tables A4.2, A4.3, A4.4, and A4.5. It is apparent that the growth of private sector health services is more important for expanding utilization in rural areas by both men and women, and again, the effects are attributable to growth of private physician practices.

Growth of the Private Sector and Choice between Private and Public Sector Providers

We next examined the relationship between the presence of private sector providers and the choice between private and public providers across the distribution of per capita expenditure. To do this, we estimated as follows:

$$PUB_{it} = PCE'_{it}\beta_1 + (PCE_{it} \bullet PRIV_{jt})\,\beta_2 + X'_{it}\alpha + d^u_{jt} + d^d + \mu_{it}, \quad (3)$$

in which PUB_{it} is an indicator of whether individual i chose a public service provider in period t. We estimate this model conditional on individuals

Table A4.2   How Does Utilization of Outpatient Services Vary with Socioeconomic Status and Access to Private Health Providers? (Urban Male Sample)

Dependent variable: visited a health provider when ill (yes = 1)	Model 1			Model 2		
	Base	× Private	Base	× Doctor	× Midwife	
Poorest 20 percent of	−0.088***	0.03	−0.088***	0.046*	−0.018	
enumeration area	[0.030]	[0.024]	[0.030]	[0.028]	[0.048]	
PCE at 2nd quintile	−0.046	0.015	−0.046	0.024	−0.007	
	[0.031]	[0.024]	[0.030]	[0.030]	[0.048]	
PCE at 3rd quintile	−0.040	−0.006	−0.040	−0.007	−0.003	
	[0.031]	[0.026]	[0.030]	[0.029]	[0.054]	
PCE at 4th quintile	−0.022	−0.031	−0.021	−0.048	0.024	
	[0.031]	[0.026]	[0.030]	[0.031]	[0.054]	
Richest 20 percent	−0.008	0.002	0.000	−0.030	0.093	
	[0.031]	[0.030]	[0.031]	[0.034]	[0.058]	
Observations	10,484			10,484		
R-squared	0.259			0.259		

Source: IFLS 1997, 2007, http://www.rand.org/labor/FLS/IFLS, estimated by authors.
Note: Standard errors in brackets. Other correlates include a year 2007 dummy, education (in years), age, age^2, age^3, age^4, gender, a dummy for urban community, and district fixed effects. PCE = per capita expenditure.
*** $p < 0.01$, * $p < 0.10$.

Table A4.3   How Does Utilization of Outpatient Services Vary with Socioeconomic Status and Access to Private Health Providers? (Urban Female Sample)

Dependent variable: visited a health provider when ill (yes = 1)	Model 1			Model 2		
	Base	× Private	Base	× Doctor	× Midwife	
Poorest 20 percent of	−0.082**	0.025	−0.082**	0.023	0.032	
enumeration area	[0.032]	[0.024]	[0.032]	[0.029]	[0.050]	
PCE at 3rd quintile	−0.070**	0.052*	−0.070**	0.055*	0.043	
	[0.032]	[0.027]	[0.032]	[0.032]	[0.052]	
PCE at 3rd quintile	−0.031	−0.034	−0.031	−0.026	−0.050	
	[0.032]	[0.024]	[0.032]	[0.030]	[0.048]	
PCE at 4th quintile	−0.002	−0.019	−0.003	−0.028	0.007	
	[0.032]	[0.026]	[0.032]	[0.031]	[0.052]	
Richest 20 percent	0.000	−0.009	−0.001	−0.033	0.052	
	[0.033]	[0.029]	[0.033]	[0.034]	[0.055]	
Observations		12,067			12,067	
		0.292			0.292	

Source: IFLS 1997, 2007, http://www.rand.org/labor/FLS/IFLS, estimated by authors.
Note: Standard errors in brackets. Other correlates include a year 2007 dummy, education (in years), age, age^2, age^3, age^4, gender, a dummy for urban community, and district fixed effects. PCE = per capita expenditure.
** $p < 0.05$, * $p < 0.10$.

Table A4.4   How Does Utilization of Outpatient Services Vary with Socioeconomic Status and Access to Private Health Providers? (Rural Male Sample)

Dependent variable: visited a health provider when ill (yes = 1)	Model 1		Model 2		
	Base	× Private	Base	× Doctor	× Midwife
Poorest 20 percent of enumeration area	0.038	0.053**	0.05	0.172***	0.027
	[0.041]	[0.025]	[0.040]	[0.057]	[0.028]
PCE at 2nd quintile	0.058	0.044*	0.074*	0.077	0.033
	[0.041]	[0.026]	[0.040]	[0.059]	[0.029]
PCE at 3rd quintile	0.073*	0.029	0.085**	0.062	0.018
	[0.041]	[0.028]	[0.040]	[0.061]	[0.033]
PCE at 4th quintile	0.069*	0.071***	0.091**	0.093	0.062**
	[0.041]	[0.025]	[0.040]	[0.060]	[0.029]
Richest 20 percent	0.128***	−0.019	0.134***	−0.059	−0.018
	[0.041]	[0.026]	[0.040]	[0.060]	[0.029]
Observations		9,321			9,321
R-squared		0.236			0.236

Source: IFLS 1997, 2007, http://www.rand.org/labor/FLS/IFLS, estimated by authors.
Note: Standard errors in brackets. Other correlates include a year 2007 dummy, education (in years), age, age^2, age^3, age^4, gender, a dummy for urban community, and district fixed effects. PCE = per capita expenditure.
*** $p < 0.01$, ** $p < 0.05$, * $p < 0.10$.

Table A4.5   How Does Utilization of Outpatient Services Vary with Socioeconomic Status and Access to Private Health Providers? (Rural Female Sample)

Dependent variable: visited a health provider when ill (yes = 1)	Model 1		Model 2		
	Base	× Private	Base	× Doctor	× Midwife
Poorest 20 percent of enumeration area	0.119***	0.059**	0.122***	0.113**	0.043
	[0.043]	[0.027]	[0.043]	[0.057]	[0.031]
PCE at 2nd quintile	0.145***	0.056*	0.148***	0.053	0.056*
	[0.043]	[0.029]	[0.043]	[0.063]	[0.034]
PCE at 3rd quintile	0.178***	0.043	0.181***	0.112*	0.020
	[0.043]	[0.028]	[0.043]	[0.058]	[0.033]
PCE at 4th quintile	0.185***	0.040	0.189***	0.011	0.044
	[0.043]	[0.027]	[0.043]	[0.059]	[0.032]
Richest 20 percent	0.235***	0.002	0.238***	0.080	−0.023
	[0.043]	[0.031]	[0.043]	[0.065]	[0.036]
Observations		10,364			10,364
R-squared		0.262			0.262

Source: IFLS 1997, 2007, http://www.rand.org/labor/FLS/IFLS, estimated by authors.
Note: Standard errors in brackets. Other correlates include a year 2007 dummy, education (in years), age, age^2, age^3, age^4, gender, a dummy for urban community, and district fixed effects. PCE = per capita expenditure.
*** $p < 0.01$, ** $p < 0.05$, * $p < 0.10$.

seeking outpatient health care services, Results are shown in table A4.6. As in (1) and (2) above, this model is estimated without a constant term to highlight the average choices by per capita expenditure quintile.

As in the examination of the effects of the private sector on utilization, the interaction terms are further expanded to examine separately the relationship between increases in the number of private sector physicians and midwives and utilization of the public sector. After the results for the entire sample in table A4.6, results from four subsamples (male urban, female urban, male rural, and female rural) are presented in tables A4.7 through A4.10.

Table A4.6   What Is the Relationship between Socioeconomic Status and the Choice between Public and Private Sector Outpatient Care? (Full Sample)

Dependent variable: uses public outpatient care (yes = 1)	Model 1	Model 2		Model 3		
	Base	Base	× Private	Base	× Doctor	× Midwife
Poorest 20 percent	0.217***	0.186***	0.081**	0.190***	0.165***	−0.045
	[0.044]	[0.046]	[0.034]	[0.046]	[0.044]	[0.054]
PCE at 2nd quintile	0.181***	0.169***	0.034	0.171***	0.048	0.012
	[0.044]	[0.046]	[0.033]	[0.046]	[0.045]	[0.050]
PCE at 3rd quintile	0.163***	0.174***	−0.039	0.175***	−0.047	−0.024
	[0.044]	[0.045]	[0.034]	[0.045]	[0.045]	[0.050]
PCE at 4th quintile	0.128***	0.127***	−0.002	0.130***	−0.075	0.068
	[0.043]	[0.045]	[0.035]	[0.045]	[0.048]	[0.049]
Richest 20 percent	0.098**	0.112**	−0.051	0.112**	−0.085*	−0.007
	[0.043]	[0.045]	[0.037]	[0.045]	[0.048]	[0.056]
Observations	8,334	8,334		8,334		
R-squared	0.467	0.468		0.467		

Source: IFLS 1997, 2007, http://www.rand.org/labor/FLS/IFLS, estimated by authors.
Notes: Standard errors in brackets. Other correlates include a year 2007 dummy, education (in years), age, age^2, age^3, age^4, gender, a dummy for urban community, and district fixed effects. PCE = per capita expenditure.
*** $p < 0.01$, ** $p < 0.05$, * $p < 0.10$.

Table A4.7   What Is the Relationship between Socioeconomic Status and the Choice between Public and Private Sector Outpatient Care? (Urban Male Sample)

Dependent variable: uses public outpatient care (yes = 1)	Model 1	Model 2		Model 3		
	Base	Base	× Private	Base	× Doctor	× Midwife
Poorest 20 percent	0.211***	0.192**	0.037	0.195**	0.150*	−0.339**
	[0.078]	[0.085]	[0.076]	[0.084]	[0.086]	[0.154]
PCE at 2nd quintile	0.110	0.058	0.125*	0.054	0.072	0.253*
	[0.078]	[0.084]	[0.068]	[0.084]	[0.086]	[0.140]
PCE at 3rd quintile	0.146*	0.133	0.024	0.130	0.017	0.044
	[0.078]	[0.085]	[0.080]	[0.085]	[0.088]	[0.152]
PCE at 4th quintile	0.088	0.097	−0.045	0.094	−0.104	0.076
	[0.078]	[0.084]	[0.076]	[0.083]	[0.092]	[0.140]
Richest 20 percent	0.029	0.026	−0.005	0.026	0.037	−0.100
	[0.079]	[0.086]	[0.084]	[0.086]	[0.096]	[0.150]
Observations	1,891	1,891		1,891		
R-squared	0.474	0.475		0.479		

Source: IFLS 1997, 2007, http://www.rand.org/labor/FLS/IFLS, estimated by authors.
Notes: Standard errors in brackets. Other correlates include a year 2007 dummy, education (in years), age, age^2, age^3, age^4, gender, a dummy for urban community, and district fixed effects. PCE = per capita expenditure.
*** $p < 0.01$, ** $p < 0.05$, * $p < 0.10$.

Table A4.8   What Is the Relationship between Socioeconomic Status and the Choice between Public and Private Sector Outpatient Care? (Urban Female Sample)

Dependent variable: uses public outpatient care (yes = 1)	Model 1	Model 2		Model 3		
	Base	Base	× Private	Base	× Doctor	× Midwife
Poorest 20 percent	0.274***	0.264***	0.025	0.264***	0.012	0.06
	[0.066]	[0.071]	[0.057]	[0.071]	[0.069]	[0.115]
PCE at 2nd quintile	0.221***	0.203***	0.043	0.203***	0.055	0.019
	[0.067]	[0.071]	[0.055]	[0.071]	[0.072]	[0.110]
PCE at 3rd quintile	0.172***	0.191***	−0.054	0.188***	−0.096	0.083
	[0.066]	[0.071]	[0.061]	[0.071]	[0.071]	[0.121]
PCE at 4th quintile	0.124*	0.119*	0.011	0.116	−0.057	0.204*
	[0.066]	[0.072]	[0.066]	[0.072]	[0.074]	[0.116]
Richest 20 percent	0.075	0.067	0.021	0.068	0.017	0.038
	[0.066]	[0.072]	[0.067]	[0.072]	[0.075]	[0.122]
Observations	2,756	2,756		2,756		
R-squared	0.478	0.479		0.480		

Source: IFLS 1997, 2007, http://www.rand.org/labor/FLS/IFLS, estimated by authors.
Notes: Standard errors in brackets. Other correlates include a year 2007 dummy, education (in years), age, age^2, age^3, age^4, gender, a dummy for urban community, and district fixed effects. PCE = per capita expenditure.
*** $p < 0.01$, * $p < 0.10$.

Table A4.9   What Is the Relationship between Socioeconomic Status and the Choice between Public and Private Sector Outpatient Care? (Rural Male Sample)

Dependent variable: uses public outpatient care (yes = 1)	Model 1	Model 2		Model 3		
	Base	Base	× Private	Base	× Doctor	× Midwife
Poorest 20 percent	−0.057	−0.124	0.215**	−0.119	0.501***	0.051
	[0.172]	[0.173]	[0.088]	[0.173]	[0.146]	[0.116]
PCE at 2nd quintile	−0.015	−0.016	−0.003	−0.016	0.106	−0.063
	[0.172]	[0.173]	[0.088]	[0.173]	[0.164]	[0.106]
PCE at 3rd quintile	−0.046	−0.036	−0.039	−0.041	0.085	−0.079
	[0.172]	[0.173]	[0.082]	[0.172]	[0.179]	[0.101]
PCE at 4th quintile	−0.034	−0.027	−0.027	−0.026	−0.069	−0.040
	[0.172]	[0.173]	[0.083]	[0.173]	[0.163]	[0.101]
Richest 20 percent	−0.018	0.001	−0.087	−0.002	−0.279	−0.041
	[0.172]	[0.173]	[0.101]	[0.173]	[0.190]	[0.123]
Observations	1,529	1,529		1,529		
R-squared	0.520	0.523		0.526		

Source: IFLS 1997, 2007, http://www.rand.org/labor/FLS/IFLS, estimated by authors.
Notes: Standard errors in brackets. Other correlates include a year 2007 dummy, education (in years), age, age^2, age^3, age^4, gender, a dummy for urban community, and district fixed effects. PCE = per capita expenditure.
*** $p < 0.01$, ** $p < 0.05$.

Table A4.10   What Is the Relationship between Socioeconomic Status and the Choice between Public and Private Sector Outpatient Care? (Rural Female Sample)

Dependent variable: uses public outpatient care (yes = 1)	Model 1	Model 2			Model 3		
	Base	Base	× Private	Base	× Doctor	× Midwife	
Poorest 20 percent	0.443***	0.465***	−0.041	0.461***	0.069	−0.100	
	[0.114]	[0.119]	[0.082]	[0.120]	[0.146]	[0.105]	
PCE at 2nd quintile	0.443***	0.482***	−0.096	0.476***	−0.142	−0.086	
	[0.114]	[0.119]	[0.079]	[0.120]	[0.149]	[0.094]	
PCE at 3rd quintile	0.429***	0.470***	−0.109	0.463***	−0.133	−0.103	
	[0.114]	[0.118]	[0.079]	[0.120]	[0.126]	[0.104]	
PCE at 4th quintile	0.389***	0.390***	0.045	0.383***	0.013	0.059	
	[0.113]	[0.118]	[0.084]	[0.119]	[0.160]	[0.100]	
Richest 20 percent	0.364***	0.404***	−0.112	0.393***	−0.271**	−0.028	
	[0.113]	[0.117]	[0.078]	[0.119]	[0.130]	[0.097]	
Observations	2,158	2,158			2,158		
R-squared	0.519	0.521			0.521		

Source: IFLS 1997, 2007, http://www.rand.org/labor/FLS/IFLS, estimated by authors.
Notes: Standard errors in brackets. Other correlates include a year 2007 dummy, education (in years), age, age^2, age^3, age^4, gender, a dummy for urban community, and district fixed effects. PCE = per capita expenditure.
*** $p < 0.01$, ** $p < 0.05$.

Table A4.11   Utilization and Quality (All Samples)

Dependent variable: individuals visit health provider when ill (yes = 1)	Female (15–49 years)		Children (0–5 years)		Adult (15 years and older)	
	Base	Interaction	Base	Interaction	Base	Interaction
Poorest 20 percent of enumeration area	−0.059	−0.014	0.04	0.017	−0.049**	0.003
	[0.041]	[0.011]	[0.063]	[0.014]	[0.020]	[0.006]
PCE at 2nd quintile	−0.037	−0.001	0.067	−0.012	−0.033	0.003
	[0.041]	[0.011]	[0.064]	[0.016]	[0.020]	[0.006]
PCE at 3rd quintile	−0.021	−0.006	0.104	0.002	−0.020	0.003
	[0.041]	[0.011]	[0.064]	[0.016]	[0.020]	[0.006]
PCE at 4th quintile	−0.009	−0.014	0.140**	−0.029	−0.014	−0.002
	[0.041]	[0.011]	[0.064]	[0.018]	[0.020]	[0.006]
Richest 20 percent	0.025	−0.015	0.176***	−0.003	0.015	−0.007
	[0.041]	[0.012]	[0.065]	[0.020]	[0.020]	[0.006]
Observations	8,601		4,427		24,628	
R-squared	0.268		0.424		0.236	

Source: IFLS 1997, 2007, http://www.rand.org/labor/FLS/IFLS, estimated by authors.
Note: Standard errors in brackets. Other correlates include year dummy, education (in years,) age, age^2, age^3, age^4, gender, and community type. Interactions in subsample of female (15–49 years), children (0–14 years), and adult (15 years and older) are, respectively, with prenatal care, child curative care, and adult curative care. PCE = per capita expenditure.
*** $p < 0.01$, ** $p < 0.05$.

Table A4.12   Utilization and Quality (Urban Sample)

Dependent variable: individuals visit health provider when ill (yes = 1)	Female (15–49 years)		Children (0–5 years)		Adult (15 years and older)	
	Base	Interaction	Base	Interaction	Base	Interaction
Poorest 20 percent of enumeration area	−0.077	−0.020	−0.057	0.023	−0.074***	0.001
	[0.049]	[0.013]	[0.087]	[0.019]	[0.025]	[0.008]
PCE at 2nd quintile	−0.067	−0.017	−0.017	−0.016	−0.056**	−0.006
	[0.049]	[0.015]	[0.088]	[0.023]	[0.025]	[0.008]
PCE at 3rd quintile	−0.068	−0.013	0.042	−0.009	−0.054**	0.001
	[0.049]	[0.014]	[0.088]	[0.022]	[0.025]	[0.008]
PCE at 4th quintile	−0.031	−0.012	0.080	−0.055**	−0.042*	−0.006
	[0.049]	[0.014]	[0.088]	[0.024]	[0.025]	[0.008]
Richest 20 percent	−0.017	−0.020	0.095	0.003	−0.011	−0.003
	[0.049]	[0.016]	[0.090]	[0.028]	[0.025]	[0.008]
Observations	4,963		2,230		12,994	
R-squared	0.283		0.468		0.234	

Source: IFLS 1997, 2007, http://www.rand.org/labor/FLS/IFLS, estimated by authors.
Note: Standard errors in brackets. Other correlates include year dummy, education (in years), age, age^2, age^3, age^4, gender, and community type. Interactions in subsample of female (15–49 years), children (0–14 years), and adult (15 years and older) are, respectively, with prenatal care, child curative care, and adult curative care. PCE = per capita expenditure.
*** $p < 0.01$, ** $p < 0.05$, * $p < 0.10$.

Table A4.13   Utilization and Quality (Rural Sample)

Dependent variable: individuals visit health provider when ill (yes = 1)	Female (15–49 years)		Children (0–5 years)		Adult (15 years and older)	
	Base	Interaction	Base	Interaction	Base	Interaction
Poorest 20 percent of enumeration area	−0.016	−0.007	0.273***	0.014	−0.004	−0.001
	[0.089]	[0.019]	[0.099]	[0.023]	[0.037]	[0.010]
PCE at 2nd quintile	0.021	0.023	0.291***	−0.004	0.011	0.010
	[0.089]	[0.019]	[0.099]	[0.024]	[0.037]	[0.010]
PCE at 3rd quintile	0.058	−0.006	0.301***	0.024	0.037	0.001
	[0.089]	[0.018]	[0.100]	[0.026]	[0.037]	[0.010]
PCE at 4th quintile	0.040	−0.016	0.338***	0.005	0.039	0.001
	[0.089]	[0.018]	[0.100]	[0.030]	[0.037]	[0.010]
Richest 20 percent	0.098	−0.012	0.403***	−0.013	0.069*	−0.013
	[0.089]	[0.019]	[0.100]	[0.031]	[0.037]	[0.010]
Observations	3,638		2,197		11,634	
R-squared	0.268		0.398		0.230	

Source: IFLS 1997, 2007, http://www.rand.org/labor/FLS/IFLS, estimated by authors.
Note: Standard errors in brackets. Other correlates include year dummy, education (in years), age, age^2, age^3, age^4, gender, and community type. Interactions in subsample of female (15–49 years), children (0–14 years), and adult (15 years and older) are, respectively, with prenatal care, child curative care, and adult curative care. PCE = per capita expenditure.
*** $p < 0.01$, * $p < 0.10$.

Notes

1. Note that the urban indicator is allowed to vary over time. This is done because some enumeration areas that were rural in 1997 were classified as urban by 2007.

2. In the regression model, private practices are represented in per thousand terms, rather than per 100,000, to facilitate readability of coefficients.

APPENDIX 5

Health Provider Knowledge and the Private Sector

To determine the effect of private sector growth, the study examined how change in the availability of private health clinics in a community is correlated with changes in diagnostic vignette scores. Variants of the following model are examined:

$$\Delta Q_{jt} = \beta_1 \Delta Priv_{jt} + \beta_2 Q_{jt-1} + \Delta X'\gamma + Sumatra + Other + \varepsilon_{jt},$$

where ΔQ_{jt} is the change in community j's vignette score from 1997 to 2007, and $\Delta Priv_{jt}$ is the change in number of private practices per 1,000 residents from 1997 to 2007. In different specifications, the effects of changing physician practices from midwife practices are examined separately. In recognition of the likely importance of convergence in quality shown earlier, a measure of the initial vignette score, Q_{jt-1}, and also a vector of changes in other community covariates, ΔX, that may independently influence quality are included. These other correlates include the medical facility utilization rate, population per square mile, log per capita expenditure in the enumeration area, a dummy variable for availability of *Askeskin/Jamkesmas* insurance in 2007, and an indicator for whether the community had an asphalt road in 2007. Finally, to control for differences in provincewide growth, dummy variables for Sumatra and Other Provinces are included.

Table A5.1   Growth of the Private Sector and Change in District Average Prenatal Care Vignette Scores, 1997–2007

Indicator	Model 1	Model 2	Model 3	Model 4
	Dependent variable: Change in prenatal care vignette score			
District average of all facilities				
Change in number of private practices per 100,000 population	0.01 [0.023]	0.018 [0.014]		
Change in number of physician practices per 100,000 population			0.084* [0.044]	0.057** [0.025]
Change in number of midwife practices per 100,000 population			−0.023 [0.020]	−0.001 [0.013]
Lag 1997 prenatal vignette score		−1.029*** [0.056]		−1.025*** [0.056]
Observations	291	291	291	291
R-squared	0.05	0.62	0.06	0.62
District average of public facilities				
Change in number of private practices per 100,000 population	−0.004 [0.022]	0.003 [0.014]		
Change in number of physician practices per 100,000 population			0.044 [0.044]	0.021 [0.026]
Change in number of midwife practices per 100,000 population			−0.026 [0.024]	−0.001 [0.014]
Lag 1997 prenatal vignette score		−1.031*** [0.054]		−1.029*** [0.054]
Observations	285	285	285	285
R-squared	0.05	0.64	0.05	0.64

Source: IFLS 1997, 2007, http://www.rand.org/labor/FLS/IFLS, estimated by authors.
Notes: Robust standard errors are in brackets. Other correlates include utilization rate, population per square mile, log per capita expenditure, indicator for *Askeskin/Jamkesmas* insurance availability in the community (yes = 1), and indicator for asphalt main road in community, all of which are at the community level and in first-differences, and two region indicators (Sumatra = 1 and Other Provinces = 1) to control for regional growth effects.
* significant at 10%; ** significant at 5%; *** significant at 1%.

The Correlations between Training and Experience and Health Provider Knowledge

Are training and experience correlated with the knowledge of health providers? It is not easy to answer the question because information on health provider knowledge and prior training is rarely found in survey data. However, the 2007 wave of the IFLS collected the information necessary to examine the association between training and knowledge. The following cross-sectional model can therefore be examined:

$$Q_j = \alpha + \beta Pub_j + Train'_j \gamma + \delta\, Exper_j + \mu^d + \varepsilon_j,$$

Table A5.2   Growth of the Private Sector and Change in District Average Child Curative Care Vignette Scores, 1997–2007

	Dependent variable: Change in child curative care score			
Indicator	Model 1	Model 2	Model 3	Model 4
District average of all facilities				
Change in number of private practices	0.006	0.001		
per 100,000 population	[0.023]	[0.018]		
Change in number of physician practices			0.078	0.069
per 100,000 population			[0.044]*	[0.031]**
Change in number of midwife			−0.026	−0.018
practices per 100,000 population			[0.033]	[0.027]
Lag 1997 prenatal vignette score		−0.871***		−0.869
		[0.060]		[0.060]***
Observations	291	291	291	291
R-squared	0.04	0.50	0.05	0.50
District average of public facilities				
Change in number of private practices	0.004	−0.005		
per 100,000 population	[0.027]	[0.020]		
Change in number of physician			0.003	0.023
practices per 100,000 population			[0.050]	[0.037]
Change in number of midwife practices			0.004	−0.002
per 100,000 population			[0.032]	[0.025]
Lag 1997 prenatal vignette score		−0.767***		−0.775
		[0.060]		[0.060]***
Observations	288	288	288	288
R-squared	0.03	0.43	0.03	0.43

Source: IFLS 1997, 2007, http://www.rand.org/labor/FLS/IFLS, estimated by authors.
Notes: Robust standard errors are in brackets. Other correlates include utilization rate, population per square mile, log per capita expenditure, indicator for *Askeskin/Jamkesmas* insurance availability in the community (yes = 1), and an indicator for an asphalt main road in community, all of which are at the community level and in first-differences, and two region indicators (Sumatra = 1 and Other Provinces = 1) to control for regional growth effects.
* significant at 10%; ** significant at 5%; *** significant at 1%.

where Q is health provider knowledge, *Pub* is dummy variable for public health provider, *Train'* is a vector of training programs that a health provider may have received during the previous 12 months, *Exper* is health provider work experience (in years), and μ^d is district fixed effect. Subscript *j* represents observations at the health provider level. As information on types of training received by health providers is only available in IFLS4 (2007), it is only possible to estimate simple contemporaneous correlations of training and experience with knowledge of health providers. District-level fixed effects are included in the estimation to control for unobserved heterogeneity, such as district-level health policies or funding that might be correlated both with opportunities to participate in training to improve knowledge and skills and with health provider knowledge.

Interpreting the parameters of interest, γ and δ, however, should be done cautiously. The estimated parameters can only be interpreted as correlations between health provider knowledge and training and experience, respectively. Potential biases, from individuals' endogenous take-up of training opportunities or from targeting of training to lower-skilled health workers, may lead to either under- or overstatement of the association between training and quality of care.

Table A5.3   What Is the Association between Training and the Prenatal Care Vignette Score?

Independent variable	Prenatal care quality			
	Percentage raw score		Scored above average (yes = 1)	
Trained in 12 months, safe delivery	0.01	0.001	0.021	0.040
(yes = 1)	[0.013]	[0.015]	[0.041]	[0.046]
Trained in 12 months, high-risk	0.003	0.012	0.004	0.007
pregnancy (yes = 1)	[0.015]	[0.017]	[0.047]	[0.053]
Trained in 12 months, labor assistance	0.000	0.003	−0.002	−0.016
(yes = 1)	[0.014]	[0.017]	[0.045]	[0.052]
Trained in 12 months, HIV transmission	0.006	0.013	0.002	−0.02
in pregnancy (yes = 1)	[0.012]	[0.013]	[0.037]	[0.041]
Trained in 12 months, obstetrical	0.003	0.003	0.021	0.035
emergency (yes = 1)	[0.012]	[0.014]	[0.038]	[0.042]
Trained in 12 months, family planning	−0.011	−0.017	0.018	0.004
(yes = 1)	[0.011]	[0.012]	[0.033]	[0.038]
Trained in 12 months, other (yes = 1)	−0.002	−0.006	−0.060	−0.060
	[0.013]	[0.015]	[0.041]	[0.046]
Health provider is public (yes = 1)		0.015**		0.039
		[0.008]		[0.024]
Work experience (years)		0.000		0.002*
		[0.000]		[0.001]
Constant	0.447***	0.440***	0.697***	0.660***
	[0.004]	[0.008]	[0.012]	[0.026]
Observations	1,877	1,537	1,877	1,537
R-squared	0.471	0.499	0.280	0.315

Source: IFLS 2007, http://www.rand.org/labor/FLS/IFLS.
Notes: Standard errors in brackets. District fixed effect is included in each specification.
*** $p < 0.01$, ** $p < 0.05$, * $p < 0.10$.

Table A5.4   What Is the Association between Training and the Child Curative Care Vignette Score?

Independent variable	Child curative care quality			
	Percentage raw score		Scored above average (yes = 1)	
Trained in 12 months, child immunization (yes = 1)	−0.001	−0.007	0.028	0.026
	[0.012]	[0.014]	[0.035]	[0.039]
Trained in 12 months, acute respiratory infection (yes = 1)	0.020	0.037**	−0.002	0.002
	[0.013]	[0.015]	[0.038]	[0.043]
Trained in 12 months, diarrhea (yes = 1)	−0.011	−0.016	−0.029	−0.034
	[0.015]	[0.017]	[0.042]	[0.047]
Trained in 12 months, malaria (yes = 1)	0.062***	0.065***	−0.033	−0.033
	[0.017]	[0.019]	[0.048]	[0.053]
Trained in 12 months, nutrition (yes = 1)	0.022*	0.015	−0.036	−0.026
	[0.013]	[0.014]	[0.037]	[0.040]
Trained in 12 months, HIV transmission in pregnancy (yes = 1)	0.021	0.019	0.010	0.008
	[0.014]	[0.016]	[0.040]	[0.044]
Trained in 12 months, prenatal care (yes = 1)	0.022*	0.022	−0.094***	−0.089**
	[0.013]	[0.014]	[0.036]	[0.041]
Health provider is public (yes = 1)		0.039***		−0.052**
		[0.009]		[0.024]
Work experience (years)		0.000		0.001
		[0.000]		[0.001]
Constant	0.612***	0.610***	0.589***	0.587***
	[0.004]	[0.008]	[0.011]	[0.024]
Observations	2,309	1,929	2,309	1,929
R-squared	0.437	0.448	0.252	0.269

Source: IFLS 2007, http://www.rand.org/labor/FLS/IFLS.
Notes: Standard errors in brackets. District fixed effect is included in each specification.
*** $p < 0.01$, ** $p < 0.05$, * $p < 0.10$.

Table A5.5   What Is the Association between Training and the Adult Curative Care Vignette Score?

Independent variable	Adult curative care quality			
	Percentage raw score		Scored above average (yes = 1)	
Trained in 12 months, diag. algorithm (yes = 1)	0.061***	0.068***	−0.029	−0.027
	[0.015]	[0.017]	[0.039]	[0.043]
Trained in 12 months, noncommunicable disease (yes = 1)	0.012	0.005	0.030	0.034
	[0.014]	[0.016]	[0.037]	[0.042]
Trained in 12 months, respiratory disease (yes = 1)	0.033**	0.018	−0.067	−0.061
	[0.017]	[0.019]	[0.043]	[0.050]
Trained in 12 months, antibiotics for respiratory disease (yes = 1)	0.027	0.035*	−0.036	−0.045
	[0.017]	[0.020]	[0.045]	[0.052]
Health provider is public (yes = 1)		0.044***		−0.132***
		[0.009]		[0.022]
Work experience (years)		0.000		0.000
		[0.000]		[0.001]
Constant	0.525***	0.522***	0.328***	0.374***
	[0.004]	[0.008]	[0.010]	[0.022]
Observations	2,199	1,824	2,199	1,824
R-squared	0.413	0.428	0.326	0.363

Source: IFLS 2007, http://www.rand.org/labor/FLS/IFLS.
Notes: Standard errors in brackets. District fixed effect is included in each specification.
*** $p < 0.01$, ** $p < 0.05$, * $p < 0.10$.

APPENDIX 6

Types of Incentives

Financial	Nonfinancial
Terms and conditions of employment: • Salary or wage • Pension • Insurance (health) • Allowances (for example, housing, clothing, child care, transportation, parking) • Paid leave	Positive work environment: • Work autonomy and clarity of roles and responsibilities • Sufficient resources • Recognition of work and achievement • Supportive management and peer structures • Manageable workload and effective workload management • Effective management of occupational health and safety risks, including a safe and clean workplace • Effective employee representation and communication • Enforced equal opportunity policy • Maternity and paternity leave • Sustainable employment
Performance payments: • Achievement of performance targets • Length of service • Location or type of work (remote locations)	Flexibility in employment arrangements: • Flexible working hours • Planned career breaks

(continued)

Financial	Nonfinancial
Other financial support:	Support for career and professional development:
• Fellowships	• Effective supervision
• Loans: approval, discounting	• Coaching and mentoring
	• Access to support for training and education
	• Sabbatical and study leave
	Access to services, such as:
	• Health
	• Child care and schools
	• Recreational facilities
	• Housing
	• Transport
	Intrinsic rewards:
	• Job satisfaction
	• Personal achievement
	• Commitment to shared values
	• Respect for colleagues and community
	• Membership of team, belonging

Source: Guidelines: Incentives for Health Professionals, joint initiative of the International Council of Nurses, International Hospital Federation, International Pharmaceutical Federation, World Confederation of Physical Therapy, World Dental Federation, and the World Medical Association, 2008, http://www.who.int/workforce alliance/documents/Incentives_Guidelines%20EN.pdf.

Bibliography

Adioetomo, S. M. 2007. "Population Projection, Demographic Bonus and its Impact on Free Basic Education in Indonesia." Consultant report, World Bank, Jakarta.

Aran, M., and M. Juwono. 2006. "Benefit Incidence of Health Expenditures in Decentralized Indonesia." Background Paper for *Making the New Indonesia Work for the Poor*, World Bank, Jakarta.

Bappenas-BPS-UNFPA. 2005. *Proyeksi Penduduk Indonesia 2000–2025* (Indonesian Population Projection). Jakarta: *Bappenas*.

Bound, J. 1991. "Self-Reported versus Objective Measures of Health in Retirement Models." *Journal of Human Resources* 26 (1): 106–38.

CFHR (Center for Health Research). 2001. "Economic Analysis – *Bidan Di Desa (BDD)* Program." Consultant report, University of Indonesia, Jakarta.

Deaton, A. S., and C. H. Paxson. 1998. "Aging and Inequality in Income and Health." *American Economic Review* 88 (2): 248–53.

Ensor, T., M. Nadjib, Z. Quayyum, and A. Megraini. 2008. "Public Funding for Community-Based Skilled Delivery Care in Indonesia: To What Extent Are the Poor Benefiting?" *European Journal of Health Economics* 9 (4): 385.

Kolehmainen-Aitken, R. L., 2004. "Decentralization's Impact on the Health Workforce: Perspectives of Managers, Workers and National Leaders." *Human Resources for Health* 2: 5.

McGarry, K. 2004. "Health and Retirement: Do Changes in Health Affect Retirement Expectations?" *Journal of Human Resources* 39 (3): 624–48.

Parliamentary Commission X. 2008. Unpublished report by Medical Education Working Group, Jakarta.

Roberts, M. J., W. Hsiao, P. Berman, and M. R. Reich. 2004. *Getting Health Reform Right: A Guide to Improving Performance and Equity.* New York: Oxford University Press.

Statistics Indonesia, BKKBN, Indonesia Ministry of Health, and Macro International. 2008. "Indonesia Demographic and Health Survey 2007: Preliminary Report." Jakarta: Statistics Indonesia, and Calverton, MD: Macro International.

Thabrany, H. 2006. "Human Resources in Decentralized Health Systems in Indonesia, Challenges for Equity." *Regional Health Forum* 10 (1): 75–88.

USAID (DRSP). 2006. "Decentralization 2006: Stock Taking on Indonesia's Recent Decentralization Reforms. Summary of Findings." Donor Working Group on Decentralization, Jakarta.

World Health Organization, United Nations Children's Fund, United Nations Population Fund, and World Bank. 2007. *Maternal Mortality in 2005.* Geneva: World Health Organization.

World Bank. 2004. "Decentralization in Indonesia's Health Sector: The Central Government's Role." Working paper 7, World Bank, Jakarta.

———. 2006. *Making Services Work for the Poor: Nine Case Studies from Indonesia.* Jakarta: World Bank.

Index

Boxes, figures, notes, and tables are indicated by *b*, *f*, *n*, and *t* following page numbers.

civil service
  midwives, employment of, 46
  physicians, employment of, 48
  reform, 4, 10, 33
contract employee program. *See* PTT
    program

D

Das, J., 19
data and methodology, 17–19, 99–100
decentralization, 3, 4, 15, 21, 32–33
definitions of health facilities and
    providers, 101–4
Demographic and Health Survey
    (2008), 72
demographics of Indonesia, 25, 26
  poverty reduction, 67n1
  underlying transitions, 11, 36–37
deployment policies, 3–4, 33–34
  policy recommendations for, 8–9
Desa Siaga (alert village) program, 46,
    55n6
diagnostic and treatment ability, 77–83
  measuring from Indonesia Family Life
      Survey vignettes, 5, 18–19, 23n6,
      76–77, 78t, 83t, 84, 85t, 87nn4–5,
      105–10, 106f
  quality of, 5, 77–83, 78t
disease prevalence, 1, 15, 37
Donabedian's definition of
    quality, 18, 23n5
dual practice, 4, 6, 8
  effect of legalization of, 35, 41, 42
  policy recommendations for, 10
  puskesmas physicians, 42, 49, 49t
  quality of health services and, 79–80
  quality of services and, 86–87

E

education and quality of health workforce
    training, 7, 21, 36, 84–85, 123–28
  accreditation and certification standards,
      7, 12, 36, 71
  adult curative care, 84, 85t, 128t
  applications to medical schools, 3
  child curative care, 84, 85t, 125t, 127t
  diagnostic ability improvements and, 79
  internships, shortage of, 7, 84
  law enacting standards for, 2
  maternal health, 5
  midwives, 54

prenatal care, 84, 85t, 124–28,
    124t, 126t
education level associated with utilization
    of health services, 60

F

family practice physicians, 5
financial protection for the poor, 2, 21–22.
    See also Askeskin/Jamkesma (health
    insurance for the poor)
focus of study, 20–22
formasi (civil service posts), 35, 37n3

G

Gadjah Mada University, 9
  Center of Health Service
      Management, 16
gender differences in utilization. *See*
    utilization of health services
general practitioners. *See also* physicians
  distribution of, xi
  emergency obstetric training for, 5
Gertler, P. J., 76
global comparisons of physician, health
    worker, and hospital bed supply
    to income, 26, 27f
Global Fund, 72
Gorontalo province, 26

H

Hammer, J., 19
Harimurti, P., 76
health education system. *See* education and
    quality of health workforce training
"Health for All" (Alma Ata Conference),
    41, 54n1
health insurance. *See* Askeskin/Jamkesma
    (health insurance for the poor)
health outcomes, 2, 25–31
  equitable access to health services
      and, 22, 22f, 30
  global comparisons, 26, 27–29f, 30t
  quality of health services and, 73–74b
Health Professional Education Quality
    project, 12–13n3, 88n6
health spending. *See* public expenditures
"Healthy Indonesia 2010," 3
hemoglobin levels, 73–74b
hospitals
  definition of, 102

ECO-AUDIT
Environmental Benefits Statement

The World Bank is committed to preserving endangered forests and natural resources. The Office of the Publisher has chosen to print *New Insights into the Provision of Health Services in Indonesia* on recycled paper with 50 percent post-consumer waste, in accordance with the recommended standards for paper usage set by the Green Press Initiative, a nonprofit program supporting publishers in using fiber that is not sourced from endangered forests. For more information, visit www.greenpressinitiative.org.

Saved:
- 4 trees
- 1 million BTU's of total energy
- 336 lbs of CO_2 equivalent of greenhouse gases
- 1,617 gallons of waste water
- 98 pounds of solid waste

green
press
INITIATIVE

www.ingramcontent.com/pod-product-compliance
Lightning Source LLC
Chambersburg PA
CBHW070922270326
41927CB00011B/2684